What people are saying about …

He Is My All

"A Bible study that can bring the brokenhearted to the Great Healer."

Francine Rivers, author of *Redeeming Love*

"Debbie Alsdorf's studies will help you affirm your identity, renew your hope, redefine your purpose, and know God as deliverer!"

Carol Kent, speaker and author of *When I Lay My Isaac Down*

"I love when I find Truth with a capital T! Debbie Alsdorf offers profound concepts in simple, easy-to-apply ways. These are the perfect Bible studies for women who've just met the Savior, or for those of us who are ready to take our relationship with Him to the next level. First page to last, *He Is My All* is a joy to read."

Liz Curtis Higgs, best-selling author of *Bad Girls of the Bible*

"Jesus said that He came to give life and give it abundantly. Debbie does a beautiful job facilitating this truth through her book. *He Is My All* will have an eternal impact on your life. Read it and be blessed!"

Denalyn and Max Lucado

"*He Is My All* served to remind me that over and over again in His Word, God assures me that He loves me with an overwhelming, everlasting, extravagant love … and it's for me! What an amazing grace!"

Angela Elwell Hunt, author of *The Tale of Three Trees* and *Uncharted*

DESIGN {4} LIVING

HE IS MY All

Living in the Truth of God's Love for Me

DEBBIE ALSDORF

David C Cook®
transforming lives together

HE IS MY ALL
Published by David C Cook
4050 Lee Vance View
Colorado Springs, CO 80918 U.S.A.

David C Cook Distribution Canada
55 Woodslee Avenue, Paris, Ontario, Canada N3L 3E5

David C Cook U.K., Kingsway Communications
Eastbourne, East Sussex BN23 6NT, England

The graphic circle C logo is a registered trademark of David C Cook.

The Web site addresses recommended throughout this book are offered as a resource to you. These Web sites are not
intended in any way to be or imply an endorsement on the part of David C Cook, nor do we vouch for their content.

ISBN 978-1-4347-6836-0
eISBN 978-0-7814-0607-9

© 2008 Debbie Alsdorf
Previously published in 2000 by Faithful Woman as *Steadfast Love* by Debbie Alsdorf. ISBN 0-7814-3384-3.

The Team: Terry Behimer, Karen Lee-Thorp, Jaci Schneider, and Susan Vannaman
Cover/Interior Design: ThinkPen Design, Greg Jackson
Cover Photo: © Richard Seagraves, Workbook Stock, Jupiter Images

Printed in the United States of America
Second Edition 2008

3 4 5 6 7 8 9 10

091914-LS

In memory of my mother,
Irene Kenzie,
who now rests in the arms of God's love

And so we know and rely on
the love God has for us.

I JOHN 4:16

CONTENTS

ACKNOWLEDGMENTS

This Bible study started as a homegrown work that was written in 1997 for the women at Cornerstc Fellowship in Livermore, California. We started with fifty eager women in September, and by Novem we had a full assembly team copying the lessons for what grew to be several hundred women doing t little homegrown study, in homes, at work, and at our church site. Since then the message has gotten i the hearts of many other women—most of whom I will never get to meet.

I want to thank the many people who have prayed and trusted God to get the message of H unchanging love into more hands and more hearts. God has used their encouragement to get t material into print and their prayers to keep it in print. I would like to thank the following for expre ing God's love to me in tangible ways:

Pastor Steve Madsen and Brenda Madsen for all the encouragement, trust, and freedom you give to serve with my heart's passion the women at Cornerstone Fellowship.

Oswald Chambers, a saint who walked the walk many years before me and has inspired my life Jesus with the words left in *My Utmost for His Highest*. My little devotional book is well-worn, and words therein much appreciated.

Betty Ellis for insisting that this material should be published and praying me through.

Voni Ribera for organizing a prayer team and remaining faithful to pray for God's work to be don

Teri Collins for sending the materials through the prison system and for encouraging me to spread news of God's love to broken women.

Diane Linse for encouragement, prayer, and organizational support with the entire Steadfast L vision and project.

Julie Smith for believing in me and paving the way for a first-time author to be published back in 20 And Terry Behimer and Don Pape for believing in this message again—and keeping it on the shelves!

The Groovy Tuesday Girls—Kim Pace, Cathy Tennyeson, Cindy Williams, Patti Esser, Nata Anderson, Teresa Burke, Beth Ann Moitoso, and our honorary Colorado member, Lorri Steer—I l being part of your lives.

My husband, Ray, for allowing me the freedom to serve the Lord through serving women.

The wonderful kids we are blessed to love: Justin and Cameron Brier, Ashley and Megan Alsdorf.

And, most especially the Lord Jesus Christ, who continues to fill me with the truth that His love me is *steadfast … fixed, firm, and unchanging. He is my All!*

Introduction

Jesus loves you, right? Most of us think that it's a no-brainer to believe that Jesus loves us. But what about taking it a step further—do you believe His love is a reality big enough to protect you, provide for you, and give you significance as a person? If you are like most women, you know it in your head, you say it with your mouth—but often that love doesn't translate well into your real, everyday life. Instead of living in the security of this mighty love, the real part of you that trudges through the daily stuff still wonders if you will ever be enough or ever do enough to make your life significant.

Most women are familiar with the dance of insecurity and are tired of living lives trying to be enough. Insecurity is a form of fear—the fear that we aren't okay. But according to Scripture, God's love drives out fear from our lives, freeing us from anything based in fear. Getting the truth of God's love into the deepest part of us is important—it's the answer to all our fears. When God's love for us begins to define our lives, we change from the inside out.

Where do you go to find the truth of God's love? You spend time in the pages of His love letters for you—*the Bible.* If you've been looking for confidence, personal worth, and healthy self-esteem, then you need to soak in His love for you. Everything starts and ends with understanding God's love. It is basic … yet powerful!

I overlooked the love of God for many years and spent much of my life living in this dance of fear and insecurity. I ended up empty, dry, and wondering if there was something more to the Christian life. I took the love of God for granted and spun my wheels trying to make myself enough through what I could do for God or how I could appear spiritual to others. Much of what defined me was not based on the truth in God's Word. I was defined by a negative image of myself, and that definition drove me. With insecurity at the helm of my life, I spent a lot of energy trying to prove myself, perfect myself, or perform perfectly for God.

I thought I understood God's love. Then I began to realize that if I really believed in His love, I would not be so afraid, anxious, and insecure. When the pieces of my life fell apart, I realized that the only thing that could put me back together again was to go deeper with God. It was in understanding the love of Jesus for me personally that I found the deep, rich walk with Him I's always wanted. I went back to the basics and started clinging to them for life, and it was there that I found all I will ever need. For it was in this place that I found the *steadfast love of God for me,* which is fixed, firm, and unchanging.

This study is more than just a book in which to neatly pen answers to questions. If you just look ι the answers, dutifully putting in your time, you will not digest all that this spiritual food was meant accomplish in your heart and mind. But if you take time to savor the words you will read in your Bibl lingering over them, enjoying them, and really tasting them, you will be experiencing what the Bible refe to as meditating on the Word of God (Ps. 119). The references you will be looking up are living and acti (Heb. 4:12), meant to be life-giving soul food, offering instruction and direction for daily living (2 Tir 3:16). When you meditate on God's Word instead of just speed-reading it, you will have an interactic with your Maker and your personal relationship with Him will come alive.

This is meant to be an interactive Bible study. In order for this to be accomplished, you mu interact with the Word of God on a personal level. This study is not for the purpose of giving you mo head knowledge. Instead, as the truth goes from head to heart, my hope is that this study will chan; your life.

The Bible is to be the manual by which we live. Manuals are practical and informative. The Bib is indeed practical as well as informative and personal. We wouldn't think of trying to operate a sewir machine with the instructions from a washing machine manual. But, for some reason we keep tryir to operate our lives with instructions other than the Word of God, which is our Maker's manual f each of us.

This study concentrates on two very important facts:

1. You were made *by* God (Ps. 139:13–16).

2. You were made *for* God (Col. 1:16).

You will know an unspeakable, unshakable peace that fills you completely when you learn to re in the God of love, who made you and has plans just for you. You will discover that you are a limite edition, God's treasure. No one on earth is exactly you.

Be sure to personalize this study all the way through. It is your journey, your experience with Go and the revelation of His love for you. I also encourage you to pray before you do each lesson. Ea time, before you begin the day's study, ask the Holy Spirit to teach you and show you the truth God's Word. Through His Spirit, God will make His Word real and applicable to you today.

I suggest you work through one lesson a week. Each lesson has a five-day format, a journaling se tion, and key points to remember. The most important thing is that you take your time and don't rus Set some time aside, even if it is just fifteen minutes to do nothing but soak in Scripture. You will ne a Bible, a dictionary, and a thesaurus. There is a section at the end of each week dedicated to journali ur thoughts, but you may want to purchase a separate journal if you need more room for processing e truths that are becoming real as you study. You may also benefit from having index cards handy to ite down verses to commit to memory that you can carry with you throughout the day.

Though this is a basic study, don't be fooled into thinking there isn't enough in it for you. These undational truths of God's Word are deep and powerful. I am daily learning more of the reality of od's love for me. This reality continues to change my life. I am praying that His love will make a amatic difference in your life too!

Wanting God's best for you,
Debbie Alsdorf

DESIGN: A PLAN, INTENT, OR A PURPOSE.

Every Design4Living resource is developed to draw women closer to Christ and to encourage intima
between a woman and her Maker. Design4Living is dedicated to helping women line up to the truth
God's Word in the practical places of everyday life. Life change and real transformation comes whe
woman's mind is renewed by the truth in God's Word. When a woman knows the truth, she is set f
to live a different life—a life designed for her by God.

4 ways to love God (Mark 12:30)

- Heart
- Soul
- Strength
- Mind

4 truths to build a foundation of stability and peace (Ps. 139)

- He Knows Me
- He Protects Me
- He Created Me
- He Values Me

4 beliefs that simplify a woman's life (Col. 1:16, Matt. 22:37–40)

- I have been Created *by* God
- I have been Created *for* God
- I have been Created to Love God
- I have been Created to Love Others

The Relationship of Love

The salvation which comes from God means being completely delivered from myself, and being placed into perfect union with Him. It means the Spirit of God has brought me into intimate contact with the true Person of God Himself. And as I am caught up into total surrender to God, I become thrilled with something infinitely greater than myself.
—OSWALD CHAMBERS

"Love the Lord your God with all your heart and with all your soul and with all your mind."
—MATTHEW 22:37

eing a Christian is not about doing all the right things, following a set of rules, or adhering to certain tuals. Being a Christian is a matter of the heart. It is all about a relationship with the God of the niverse and the Creator of all things. Relationship with God is an intimate, up-close-and-personal lationship with the One who knows me most—and loves me still.

Religion is a belief in a supernatural power and an adherence to a set of rules and regulations. *elationship* is the connection with that power. While religion is the head knowledge of spiritual ings, relationship is the heart, connecting with the things of the spirit. It is possible to be religious hile not having any personal relationship with God. This kind of religious experience is empty and ustrating.

Many people grow up in homes that teach religion in some form or another. I did. I grew up in a ome where Sunday church attendance was an absolute priority, but we never talked about God in ur home except during a small handful of emergencies. Then we would say our memorized prayers and y our eyes out to God for help. But once the crisis was over and we were back to the daily business of

living, God was out of sight and out of mind. He seemed far away, perched up on a cloud somewhe
watching to see if I was being a good little girl.

Because my family went to church, I guess I had religion. I know I didn't have a relationship wi
God. I had no idea what it meant to connect with God or have my life tied into Him and His plar
My life was all about my plans and my dreams. I had no idea that God had plans for my life and th
finding purpose in Him would be more fulfilling than all my own dreams.

To many of us God sometimes seems far away and removed from real life. But I've come to lea
that He is interested in and involved with every one of us each day. I now know that He has given

> Come, let us return to the
> LORD.... He will heal us ...
> he will bind up our wounds....
> He will revive us ... he will
> restore us, that we may live in
> his presence (Hos. 6:1–2).

access to a personal relationship with Himself through H
Son, Jesus Christ. First Timothy 2:5–6 tells us, "For there
one God and one mediator between God and men, the ma
Christ Jesus, who gave himself as a ransom for all men."

Do you have a personal relationship with God through F
Son, Jesus? This may sound like a basic question, but it is a
important one. This is not a trick question. You obviously knc
with whom you have relationships. Don't misunderstand the question. I am not asking, "Do you go
church?" I am asking you, "Do you know Jesus? Do you know who He was, why He came, what F
taught, and who He is today?" This is a question of relationship with God, and it is a personal questio

Perhaps you have been a Christian for many years, but still deep inside you are frustrated, hui
ing, insecure, and anxious much of the time. You keep thinking that your belief in God should I
making a difference in your life. Let me ask you a question: Do you have *a love relationship with Go*
I am not referring to the decision that leads to salvation or the completion of religious achievemen
or rituals. Rather, I am asking if you have the daily connection with God that makes Him Lord ar
Master of your life.

 DAY ONE: UP CLOSE AND PERSONAL

There is a big difference between knowing about God in your head and experiencing God in the ve
depths of your ordinary, everyday existence. Experiencing God requires relationship—a love relatio
ship of the heart. Perhaps it has been a long time since you have been that up close and personal wi

m. Or perhaps you have never known that you could be. In this close personal relationship with
d we experience healing, restoration, and the ultimate peace we all long for.

What do you think it means to have a relationship with God?

Read Hosea 6:1–2.

According to this passage, when we return to God what does He do? (Keep in mind that *revive* means to bring
back to life and strength. *Restore* means to bring back to an original state by repairing or rebuilding.)

Our original state was "naked and unashamed."[1] Today when we are in relationship with God, we
ve the freedom to be real with ourselves and with others, unashamed of our weaknesses, embracing
s healing and strength. But we have all been wounded in real
e and have at times traveled far from that original state of close
rsonal fellowship with God. When away from God we become
aid[2] and try desperately to cover ourselves. We hide behind
asks while covering up the beauty God created in us. When
come back into relationship with Him, He heals our wounds
d brings us back to spiritual life again. Returning is something we should do each day when we wake
—returning again to the Lord, day by day.

> What is a relationship? It is an association between two or more things; a connection, interdependence, link; a tie in, hook up.[3]

Have you ever pondered the significance of the simple phrase, "God loves you"? It may embody the most important truth anyone can grasp: that God has called us into a loving relationship with Himself. Our part is simply to trust and believe in the deep care and compassion God freely extends to us. How beautiful it is to experience the freedom and joy of a love relationship with God! [4]

—CHUCK SMITH

- Look up *presence* in the dictionary and write out the definition.

- When you return to God, He enables you to live in His presence. How does the definition you j wrote help you understand the meaning of living in God's *presence*?

- What would living in God's presence 24/7 mean to you personally? What would change?

Living in God's presence is living in the state of believing He is always present with us, actively work and alive in us. It is living with the constant remembrance of Jesus, who lived to please the Fath It is living to do those things we know God loves, because we love Him and have a relationship w Him. It is not living by a set of rules but rather by the code of a heart in tune with its Maker.

3. Read Hosea 6:3. Write out the key words.

- How do you acknowledge the Lord in your life?

Yes, let us know (recognize, be acquainted with, and understand) Him; let us be zealous to know the Lord [to appreciate, give heed to, and cherish Him] (Hos. 6:3 AB).

This Bible study is about knowing God. It about being acquainted with Him. It is about goi from a "crisis relationship" with Christ to an "eve day relationship." Many of us are not connected

im, even after years of being Christians. Some of us are connected to programs, ministries, theolo-
es, and good works, but we are still not connected to God. Sadly, many of us do not understand His
ve, and therefore we serve out of obligation, fear, or a desire to please people, rather than serving out
f a love relationship with our Maker.

> *Activity, though essential to practical faith, is not a substitute for personal fellowship. It can*
> *never outweigh intimacy with God. Our relationship with Christ erodes and cools when our*
> *primary focus is taken off the Messiah and placed on other things. That is the beginning of*
> *idolatry, and it is a dangerous path for the saint to tread. The gods of this age—sports, work,*
> *money—are cleverly disguised and ensnare many Christians with their compelling allegiance.*
> *Too much of a good thing can be wrong if it distracts you from devotion to Christ.*[5]
>
> —Charles Stanley

First love (priority love) gives God first place. On a scale of 1–10, what place does a relationship with
God rank in your life? Why?

How would you describe your present relationship with God?

Write out Psalm 139:3.

Write out Psalm 139:23–24.

In Psalm 139:3 we see clearly that God had a relationship with David. God was familiar with of David's ways. In the same way God is familiar with us. In verses 23–24 we read more about David relationship with God. David trusted God to search the deepest part of him, exposing anything th would be unhealthy to his spiritual growth. Like David, we also can have this sort of relationship wi God. It is a personal interaction that is not dependent on another's actions, approval, or faith. It is o personal interaction and experience with God.

Lord,
Work in me as I seek to know how real You are and how much You love me. Build our relationship and create in me new eyes to see Your Word as fresh truth. Amen.

> *… that is the greatest joy in life—to experience a genuine love relationship with God. To know that He is for us, that He loves us, is the greatest source of security any person will ever know. Discovering the glorious grace of God was one of the most important events in my whole spiritual experience. I learned to relate to God on an entirely new basis: not on the basis of my works, or of my righteousness, but on the basis of God's love for me through Jesus Christ.[6]*
>
> —CHUCK SMITH

 DAY TWO: THE MOST EXCELLENT WAY

1. Read 1 Corinthians 13.

- Paul introduces this chapter by saying, "And now I will show you the most excellent way" (1 Cc 12:31). What do you think Paul means by that statement?

- According to 1 Corinthians 13:2–3, what do you gain by good works or spiritual gifts alone? Why

In 1 Corinthians 13:2, we see Paul expressing that even if he had all knowledge and great faith would be nothing without the love of God. How often we search for things that will make us seem ɔre knowledgeable, more spiritual, and more enviable. Even as Christians we turn to people and ings much more readily than we turn to God. Often we bypass God's love as if it were some fluffy tra we don't need. We get down to the real work of serving and doing things for God. In reality He most interested in who we are on the inside. What I do for God is not nearly as important as who m with God. There is a big difference. Embracing His love, understanding that God is love, is the ɔst excellent way to live.

Often we only look at 1 Corinthians 13 as a list of ways we are to behave, and we use it to generate a of rules. We conclude that we are to be more patient, kind, etc. Right now I encourage you to look at s chapter as the characteristics of *God's love toward you.* Don't look at who you need to be, look at who ɔd is. This is personal.

You may feel as if you have blown it big time, and that there is no hope. But then you read 1 Corinthians :5: "God keeps no record of wrongs." I hope you will begin to be filled with hope and absolute adoration this God who is so tender, loving, and forgiving.

Make a list of the characteristics of God's love toward you as outlined in 1 Corinthians 13:4–7.

:OD'S LOVE IS:	HOW GOD SHOWS HIS LOVE TO ME:
atient	*He is always patient with me when I*

• What characteristic of God's love means the most to you today? Explain.

• What does love *never* do? (See 1 Corinthians 13:8.)

2. Write out Lamentations 3:21–23.

• What is "new every morning" for you?

> Lord, I am so grateful that each day is new with You. So often I sit in shame or discouragement over my past and my mistakes, but Your Word says Your mercies are new each day, and that Your love will never fail. Help me to believe this in the depths of my soul. Amen.

 DAY THREE: GIVING GOD ALL OF ME

1. Read 1 Chronicles 28:20.

• David had given his son Solomon a task. What was to be Solomon's attitude toward what now ahead of him?

Why could he have this attitude?

What was the promise?

What did God promise not to do in any circumstance?

Now back up to 1 Chronicles 28:9–10. This chapter records David's plans for the temple and David's instruction to his son Solomon regarding the temple. God called Solomon to build something important—a sanctuary. In order for Solomon to complete the work, he had to be strong. We see in verse 9 some keys to the type of love relationship with God that would produce strength for everything Solomon was called to do. These keys will also give us the strength for all that God has planned for us.

Write your thoughts on each of the following key sentences, taken from 1 Chronicles 28:9–10.
Acknowledge God

Serve Him with your whole heart

Serve Him with devotion

Serve Him with a willing mind

Seek Him

When you are in a relationship with God, you will become strong and secure, because you w
realize that He is with you and will never fail you. His love is new every morning, and that is enou
to give all of us courage and joy! But … how do we get all this wonderful stuff from our heads to o
hearts and then into our everyday lives?

Here are our instructions:

"If you *seek him*, he will be found by you" (1 Chron. 28:9).

"He will restore us, that we may *live in his presence*" (Hos. 6:2).

3. Write out James 1:5.

4. Write out Matthew 7:7.

We must ask God to make His Word real to us and applicable to our lives. When we knock in pray
we can be sure the door will open! This is a relationship of communicating with the Father. This is a rel
tionship built by relying on Him, asking Him for wisdom, seeking His will, and knocking in prayer.

Lord,
I come to You for a relationship that is authentic. As a child trusts a parent, so
I long to trust fully in You. I am broken in some areas and need to learn how
to trust Truth. Amen.

DAY FOUR: FROM HEAD TO HEART

Read 1 Corinthians 2:11–16.

What do these verses say to you about transferring God's truth from your head to your heart?

According to these verses, who can make the truth of God's love real to you?

According to the last verse, what do you have? What does that mean?

Read John 14:15–18. Who is with you forever?

Read John 15:26. What does the Spirit do?

Read John 16:5–14. How does the Spirit bring glory to Jesus?

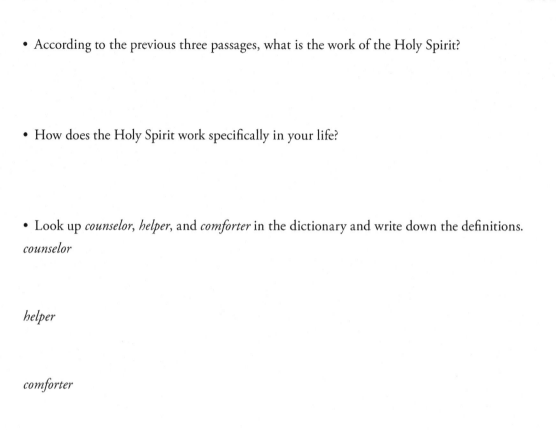

• According to the previous three passages, what is the work of the Holy Spirit?

• How does the Holy Spirit work specifically in your life?

• Look up *counselor*, *helper*, and *comforter* in the dictionary and write down the definitions.
counselor

helper

comforter

Have you ever prayed and asked God to pour out the power of the Holy Spirit on you, to gu
you into the truth of God's love just for you?

Asking for the wisdom of the Holy Spirit to make God's love real and personal to you must b
starting point if you are going to experience the love of God in your daily life. I am excited to kn
that God has provided a Helper, Teacher, and Counselor for me in the Holy Spirit. While the worl
busy connecting to philosophies, I know that I can connect with the Spirit of the living God.

All this is made possible by receiving Him: "Yet to all who received him, to those who believed
his name, he gave the right to become children of God—children born not of natural descent, nor
human decision or a husband's will, but born of God" (John 1:12–13).

I am His child, and He wants to teach me things about life, about love, and about Himself. Wh
others are still searching for something to guide them, I can be assured that I have the best and m
accurate Guide around—the Spirit of God!

The Holy Spirit can and will make God's love real to you. Pray the Word of God, as written in John 16:13. Your prayer might look something like this:

Father,
Thank You that Your Word says Your Spirit leads me into all truth. I ask You to lead me into an understanding of Your love for me and guide me into all truth regarding my value and purpose in Your plan. I ask You to do this by the power of Your Spirit. Amen.

Write out 1 Corinthians 2:12.

Do you believe God's love has been freely given to you? Why, or why not?

How can the Holy Spirit give you fresh perspective and insight in this area?

Write out Deuteronomy 6:4–5.

Look up *treasure* in a dictionary. What does it mean?

• Look up *possession*. What does it mean?

Lord,
It is amazing to think that Your love for me is at the level of declaring that I am Your treasure and Your possession. Help me to understand the truth that I am Yours, and that Your love for me signifies the worth You have imparted to me by creating me in Your image. Amen.

 DAY FIVE: GETTING A LIFE BY EMBRACING GOD'S LOVE

1. Read Philippians 1:9. Copy this part of Paul's prayer.

• What does Paul say you need regarding love?

We cannot understand God's love and enter into a relationship with Him on our own. We nee the Spirit of God to teach us and give us depth of insight.

Our world uses many different things as markers of success and value. We need to understand Goc marker of value and success if we are going to truly succeed. A relationship with God is God's marker success. Psalm 1 says in part, "Blessed is the [woman] who delights in the … LORD…. Whatever [she] do prospers." (That is a successful woman!) We must pray to become lovers of God rather than lovers of mer

2. Read John 5:39–40. What are your thoughts regarding this passage?

Do you think you have refused to come to God for "life"? Why, or why not?

You can have biblical knowledge coming out of your ears, but if you haven't come to God and nnected with Him, you still need to *Get a Life!*

> *It is the most profound common sense of all to put our poor, weak, foolish and helpless*
> *selves into the care and keeping of God who made us, who loves, us, and who alone can*
> *care for us. When we yield to God, it means we then belong to God, and that we now*
> *have all His infinite power and infinite love at work on our side! What I am inviting you*
> *to do is this: yield yourself to Him. Take advantage of this amazing privilege that human*
> *words cannot even express … regardless of circumstances or consequences … yield.*[7]
>
> —HANNAH WHITALL SMITH

In the early church it was a definite characteristic of spiritual deficiency if people lived to please her people rather than to please God. That is why Jesus said His fellow countrymen didn't have e love of God in their hearts (John 5:42). The religious people of that time had plenty of rules and gulations that governed their relationship with God. These rules all came tumbling down when Jesus luced everything to one twofold command: Love God with all your heart, soul, strength, and mind; d love your neighbor as yourself.

Many of you may have been turned off by rules in the church. Maybe Christ represents only rules you. Well, Jesus Christ wants to represent love and life. This life is not about following man-made les, but about following God.

Read Revelation 2:1–5.

When two people fall in love there is a thrill in the new relationship. And when we come to Christ ere is a thrill in our newfound forgiveness and the knowledge of God's love for us. What happens to e thrill of that love relationship with God? We get busy, don't we? Just like the church in Ephesus,

we mean well, we serve hard for God, but in the middle of running ourselves ragged to be all we c
for Christ, we lose the most important thing—relationship!

• What does Christ tell us to do in this passage as we learn from the exhortation to the church
  Ephesus?

• What did Christ hold against them? Why?

Height: the highest
point, the point of
greatest intensity.
}
• What did He call it? The _____ from which they h
  _____.

4. Write out Matthew 22:37–38.

I encourage you this week to concentrate on what it means to have a relationship with God. W
does it mean to love Him with all your being? Maybe t

May the words of my mouth and
the meditation of my heart be
pleasing in your sight, O Lord,
my Rock and my Redeemer
(Ps. 19:14).
}
concept is new to you, or maybe God is using this study
take your current relationship with Him to new levels
commitment and surrender. Wherever you are in your re
tionship to God, be sure to ask Him to keep you from thir
that hinder your love and devotion to Him. Ask Him da

to fill you with the desire to love Him with all that is within you.

A spiritual journey isn't about "arriving" or finally "getting it together." We never arrive ur eaven! But we can always be growing. Growth is active—alive with hope and promise. Each new ay we can be slowly and steadily deepening our connection to God.

In every circumstance remember that God is with you. With each step, remember He is along- de you. He is not far off and unable to hear you or see you. He is closer to you than you realize. is presence is real. All He claims to be is real.

Let's remember to make the connection with God, inviting Him into our most personal oughts and dreams. Ask His direction for living the Bible as if the pages were the blueprints for r life's design.

There is a difference between memorizing Scripture and thinking biblically. There's a difference between knowing the words and experiencing their meaning. There is a difference between having sentences embedded in your head and having their impact embedded in your heart. There is a difference between "doing Christianity" and being a Christian. You can memorize all the words, but if you've forgotten the music you still won't be able to sing the song.[8]

—TIM HANSEL

Dear Lord,

May I be Your woman, from the inside out. May I never forget the music of Your love for me. Keep me from just doing things that have the look of spirituality. Instead, give me the gift of experiencing Your Spirit on a daily basis. Thank You for Your love. Thank You that I am Your child. Thank You for Your faithfulness and Your love that is new every morning. Amen.

Journal Page

- Think back on the time in your life when you were caught in the fresh thrill of knowing and lovi Christ. What did that look like? If it has changed, how has it? What can bring you back to the lo you knew at first?

- Being a Christian is not about me being "good"; it is about receiving the goodness of God through Jesus Christ.
- Religion and relationship are as different as night and day. God calls me to relationship.
- To have relationship with God I must return and acknowledge Him.
- When I am acknowledging Christ I begin to live in His presence daily.
- Living in God's love is the most excellent way to live; it's a new and better way.
- Being a Christian is about surrendering my life to Christ for His purposes.
- The Holy Spirit works in the life of the believer as a Helper and Counselor.
- Scripture declares that I am a woman belonging to God, His treasured possession.
- I can do many things "for" the Lord, but "being" in a love relationship with Him is what counts.

God Is Love

LESSON 2

God is love. Whoever lives in love lives in God, and God in him.

—1 JOHN 4:16

In 1 John 4:16 we read that "God is love." It doesn't say that He loves, although we know that God does love us with unconditional love. This verse says that God *is* love. This is His nature, who He is. He will never be anything other than love because to be so would be contrary to His own nature.

Love is such a loose term these days that we often don't know what it really means. It can refer to anything from a vague impression to the most sincere depth of emotion and commitment. We live in a time with a confused concept of love. We have grown up with fairy-tale love and false expectations and dreams. We have picked up mixed messages of love.

That's why it is so important to have our minds renewed by God's Word. We need to be asking ourselves, "What does the Bible say about love?"

We love many things. I love my family, shopping, having fun with friends, my darling little dogs Bubba and Molly … and, of course, chocolate. (Doesn't every woman love chocolate?!) Love's range is widespread. That is one of the reasons why it's hard for us to believe the depth of God's character when we read that He is love and that He loves us. We often reduce His love to a generality instead of embracing it as the life-affirming truth that it is.

In this lesson we will begin looking closely at God's nature of love. We will examine it and thir about how it affects us in a personal and practical way. I encourage you to focus only on your relatio ship to that love. This lesson's focus is not on you loving others or any performance relating to lov Instead, this lesson encourages you to breathe in a deep fresh breath of God's love *just for you.* Let the lesson be personal! Let it be a building block in your relationship with God. Your trust in God's lo nature is critical. It is my prayer that as you complete this lesson, you will come to understand mo fully that God is Love, and that He always works in and through your life with that love.

   DAY ONE: HIS LOVE ENDURES FOREVER

1. Read Psalm 117. Write it out.

• Psalm 117 has only two verses, but those two verses contain a powerful message. What are the tw things this psalm says about God's relationship toward you? Personalize this!

• What does this psalm tell you to do?

(Note: *Extol* means to praise God highly. How do we do that? Well, in everyday terms that wou mean thanking Him, honoring Him, worshipping Him, speaking and singing to Him—declaring H goodness!)

• Is the message of His enduring love encouraging to you? How, or why not?

Some people find it hard to grasp the message of God's love. Life is not always easy, and we are often disappointed with the way things turn out in our lives. Sometimes we blame our circumstances, sometimes we blame others, and often we blame ourselves. At times we even blame God. Some blame God openly, and others silently hide their disappointment. How many times the Lord must have heard, "If You really are a God of love, why did You let this happen?" or "You are God! You could have prevented this!"

It's easy to doubt God's love when the days are discouraging and life is tough. But God's love never changes. Our circumstances change and our emotions change, but God never does. When you begin to question God's love, stop and encourage yourself with the truth. Settle the truth of God's love in your heart and mind. He created you for a love relationship, one in which He always acts in love toward you. For Him to act otherwise would be a contradiction of who He is. He deals with our lives in a personal, loving fashion. We must respond with a personal interaction and relationship. No one can interact with the Lord for you. It's your relationship.

> Certain things no one can do for you…. You don't say, "I'm in love with that wonderful person, but romance is such a hassle. I'm going to hire a surrogate lover to enjoy the romance in my place. I'll hear about it and be spared the inconvenience." Who would do that? Perish the thought. You want the romance firsthand. You don't want to miss a word or a date, and you certainly don't want to miss the kiss, right? Certain things no one can do for you.[1]
> —MAX LUCADO

Every dealing God has had with you is an expression of love. If you really believe that God's nature is love, you will accept that His will and way in your life is love. Even when things happen that you don't understand, you can be assured that He has not left you even for a moment. His love is with you even in the darkest tunnel, the most frightening storm, and in the stillness of loneliness.

His will and way in your life is always best. He isn't a God of second best when we walk in His ways. If you have trouble settling this in your heart, ask God to show you what is keeping you from believing wholeheartedly in His love. Don't be afraid to take the dark bits of your heart to Him.

I have called upon You, O God, for You will hear me; incline Your ear to me and hear my speech. Show Your marvelous loving-kindness, O You Who save by Your right hand those who trust and take refuge in You from those who rise up against them. (Ps. 17:6–7 AB).

Many of us have worn-out faith. Our faith has become depleted from the hardships and disa
pointments of life. We struggle to believe that God is the loving Father the Bible says He is.
struggle when we expect God to be some Fairy Godfather in the sky, supplying all our dreams a
wishes. Often we are so focused on what we want out of life—our plans, circumstances going our w
our goals and dreams, other people and their approval, or things—that we neglect to focus on knowi
God and forget to pray that His will be done in our lives. When things to wrong, we fall apart and r
from the love God has for us. We become disappointed, depleted, and worn out.

Have you been blaming yourself, others, or God? Perhaps it's time to ask Him to teach you abc
His love for you and His way of looking at life.

3. Read Psalm 17:6–7. What adjectives are used to describe God's love?

• Do you want to *know* the wonder of His great love? Why, or why not?

• Look up *wonder* in the dictionary. Write the definition here.

• Look up *great* in the dictionary and write the definition.

It is a remarkable thing that God loves us. We are imperfect. We fail and are often rebellious a
weak. But God's love doesn't depend on our goodness at all. In fact, thinking we are "good" can
a trap that keeps us from further understanding God's love. Because God's love is not based on c
performance, His love is an excellent thing … a surprise … a marvel. It is a wonder!

His love is great! I love this definition of *great:* "much above average in size, amount, or intensity." nother definition of *great* is: "important." Using those definitions, we can read Psalm 17:7 this way: Show the wonder of your *important* love." Or we can read it: "Show the wonder of your love that is ove all average loves … more intense, bigger than any other, and more important than any love I ave ever known or will ever know."

Lord,
Great is Your love! Help me embrace this at the most practical places in my life. Amen.

DAY TWO: FROM THE INSIDE OUT

Read Ephesians 3:16–19. This is Paul's prayer for the church in Ephesus. What does verse 16 say Paul desired for the Ephesians?

What power can strengthen you in your inner being?

Write out Psalm 109:21–22.

Stop right now and call on God as David did in the psalm above. Communicate with Him about ur hurts and needs. Have you been disappointed, or are you stuck in a rut of worn-out faith? Tell od about your heart, its condition, and its need for His love.

3. Write out Ephesians 3:16.

Stop right now and pray this for yourself. Ask the Lord, out of His glorious riches, strengthen you with power through His Spirit in your inner being.

> *The scripture plainly teaches that the gift of the Holy Spirit is a universal gift to all believers.... We must believe, therefore, that this unspeakable gift, which is meant to help us enter into the glorious realms of the Spirit now, is already the possession of even the weakest and most failing child of God. It is true, whether we recognize His presence or not, whether we acknowledge and obey His control or not. He is within each of us.... The secret is that we must allow Him to take full possession. We are His sanctuary, His dwelling place, although we may not yet have opened every inward chamber of our hearts to let Him dwell therein ... simply recognize the presence of God already within you, and fully submit to His ownership, and allow Him to control every circumstance.[2]*
>
> —Hannah Whitall Smith

The Message paraphrases Ephesians 3:16–20 this way:

> *I ask him to strengthen you by his Spirit—not a brute strength but a glorious inner strength—that Christ will live in you as you open the door and invite him in. And I ask him that with both feet planted firmly on love, you'll be able to take in with all followers of Jesus the extravagant dimensions of Christ's love. Reach out and experience the breadth! Test its length! Plumb the depths! Rise to the heights! Live full lives, full in the fullness of God. God can do anything, you know—far more than you could ever imagine or guess or request in your wildest dreams! He does it, not by pushing us around but by working within us, his Spirit deeply and gently within us.*

Note: If you have never written in a spiritual journal, this would be a wonderful time

gin. Often when we write out our feelings and prayers, it helps us to define where we are and
hat God is speaking to us personally. You may want to get a book to journal in. It can be a
etty book that is sold at a stationery store or it can be a simple spiral binder. You should keep
ur book handy to write in each time you sit down to read the Bible. Then you can jot down
rses and what they mean to you. You can also record what God is speaking to your heart that
y. There is no right or wrong in what you might write, so fill your blank pages with prayers,
ripture, poems, wishes, and dreams—or whatever God is quietly speaking just to you.

 DAY THREE: CHRIST DIED FOR ORDINARY PEOPLE

Write out 1 John 3:16. How would you describe this kind of love?

Write out and reflect on Romans 5:8. Make notes on your thoughts.

Write out and reflect on 1 John 4:9–10.

Write out and reflect on 1 John 4:15–16. On what does this verse say you should know and rely?

• According to 1 John 4:15–16, what describes God?

Lord,
I don't want to just have a head full of Jesus—I want a heart full of Jesus.
Make that so. Amen.

 DAY FOUR: THE CONNECTION

1. Write out John 15:9. (These are the words of Christ … love those red letters!)

• According to John 15:9, where are you to remain?

If we are to remain "in" something, we must pray to understand what that means. According the dictionary, *remain* means "to continue without change; to stay after the removal or loss of othe to be left as still to be dealt with; to endure/persist."

Throughout this study I will be referring to three *Rs:*

Remain in God. How do we remain in His love? (Read John 15:10–11.) This is a key to living ea day in a personal relationship with the Father.

Renew yourself in Him daily. Romans 12:2 says, "be transformed by the renewing of your min Our minds should be renewed with the words of truth found within the pages of the Bible.

Rest. Philippians 4:6–7 tells us, "Do not be anxious about anything, but in everything, by pra and petition, with thanksgiving, present your requests to God. And the peace of God, which tra scends all understanding, will guard your hearts and your minds in Christ Jesus." Peace is rest!

Whenever I am out of sorts, I like to use the *Rs* as a check system.

Am I **remaining** today? Am I connected, abiding in Christ?

Am I **renewed** today? Have I read or meditated or thought about His Word?

Am I **resting** today? Have I prayed and turned my life over to God?

Usually one of the *Rs* will be missing, sometimes all of them. Then I need to go back to God and connect with Him. That is what it is all about—a connection with God.

We read the Word, we pray. We connect, and we rest in Jesus. We will never understand the love of God unless we get to know Him through His Word and through a personal relationship with Him.

Write out John 3:16.

Now personalize this verse in your heart by writing it with your own name:

For God so loved _____

Remember Matthew 22:37 from lesson 1? Write out that verse again here.

God created us to long for Him with every part of us: heart, soul, strength, mind.

- Heart—the things of the spiritual life
- Soul—the things of the emotional life
- Strength—the things of the physical life
- Mind—the things of the thought life

When all four to come together under God's rule they create balance.

4. Read Ecclesiastes 3:11–14. What has God set in the hearts of men?

• What does this mean?

The reason there is always a longing within us is that God has set eternity in our hearts—somethi
beyond just living for ourselves. We were created to find satisfaction in the living God and His etern
plans and purposes. We were created to know Him, to love Him, to surrender to Him, and then
serve Him. This is to long for God with every part of us.

But from the beginning of time, people have sought to "do what they want to do" and in
doing, have become lost in the self-life. In this place we become divided in our hearts, and God
longer is the greatest love in our lives.

> Lord,
> Help me to remember each day that connection to You is the most important
> thing—the first call of duty in my day. It doesn't have to be a programmed time
> but can be a freeing and natural relationship with You that begins the moment
> I wake and continues until I lay my head down again at night. Amen.

 DAY FIVE: BEFORE I SOUGHT GOD, HE SOUGHT ME

1. Write Romans 5:8 in your own words.

The sacrificial love of Jesus Christ is a type of love that is foreign to us. It's hard for us to comprehend conditional love, because we live in a world of conditions. It's hard for us to love those who don't love , who disappoint us, hurt us, or ultimately fail us. But Christ in His goodness has the Ultimate Love, at while we were plain "yuck" He died for us. And the best news is that this same love protects and ablishes us all the days of our lives. Isaiah 45:22 says, "Turn to me and be saved." Don't mull around your "stuff," trying to figure out how God could possibly save you, just look to Him.

Many of us have a mental picture of what a Christian should be, and looking at this image in other Christian' lives becomes a hindrance to our focusing on God. This is not salvation—it is not simple enough. He says, in effect, "Look to Me and you are saved," not "You will be saved someday." We will find what we are looking for if we will concentrate on Him. We get distracted from God and irritable with Him while He continues to say to us, "Look to Me, and be saved...." Our difficulties, our trials, and our worries about tomorrow all vanish when we look to God. Wake yourself up and look to God. Build your hope on Him. No matter how many things seem to be pressing in on you, be determined to push them aside and look to him. "Look to Me...." Salvation is yours the moment you look.[3]

—OSWALD CHAMBERS

Do you realize that His Spirit is working deeply d gently within you today? It is His desire that we ow His love, and it is His desire that we look to Him ch day. The love of Jesus Christ must be the founda- n of our lives. In knowing this love, we have peace d fullness and are able to be vessels through which od's love can ultimately be poured out to others, bringing them into the knowledge of Jesus Christ.

This love holds nothing back, but, in a manner which no human mind can fathom, makes thee one with itself. Oh wondrous love, to love us even as the Father loved Him, and to offer us this love as our everyday dwellings![4] —Andrew Murray

Pick the Scripture verse that spoke to you the most from this week. Write it here and then memorize it this coming week. You may also want to write it on an index card and carry it with you as a reminder.

Tell yourself the following truth this week: God's love is fixed, firm, unchanging. His love i

reality of my life.

I love You fervently and devotedly, O Lord, my Strength. The Lord is my Rock, my Fortress, and my Deliverer; my God, my keen and firm Strength in Whom I will trust and take refuge, my Shield, and the Horn of my salvation, my High Tower. (Ps. 18:1–2 AB).

Dear Lord,

May I know Your love in a way unlike I have ever known it before. I desire to remain in that same love that first loved me and sought me out while I was turned the other way. By the power of Your Spirit, may I remain in You, renew myself in You, and rest in You … as You fill me each day with the indwelling of Yourself. Amen.

Journal Page

Do you compare yourself to other women? Do you compare your life and your spirituality to theirs? How does that affect you?

KEY POINTS FROM LESSON 2

- God's love for me endures forever.
- His love is great; it is a wonder.
- God's will is to change me from the inside out.
- God desires to strengthen me with the power of His Spirit.
- He does this so that Christ may dwell in my heart by faith.
- His will is that I be rooted and established in love.
- God Himself will fill me to the measure of all fullness through Christ.
- Christ died for ordinary people—like me.
- To fulfill God's plan I must be connected to Christ daily.
- I am to remain in God, through daily relationship with Christ.
- I am to renew daily through His Word—which is truth and freedom.
- I am to rest in what is true about His involvement in my life and refuse worry.
- Before I ever sought God, He was coming after me. He has called me to be His.

Love Is Real and Practical

LESSON 3

Keep your life so constantly in touch with God that His surprising power can break through at any point. Live in a constant state of expectancy, and leave room for God to come in as He decides.
—OSWALD CHAMBERS

The LORD Almighty is with us.
—PSALM 46:7

ᴇ most practical thing you can do is to learn about God and seek to understand how He desires
ᵉal, practical, and personal relationship with you. God is not far off, removed from your life, and
ᵢconcerned. The God of Scripture is a God who related to people in very real ways. When we reduce
ᵓd's love to a bumper sticker slogan, we miss the meaning of this real and everyday practical relation-
ᵢp we can have with Him. He is present with us, and we can experience Him fully.

The word love has fallen on bad times. To many people it means nothing more nor less than
going to bed with somebody, never mind what sex the other may belong to. Bumper stickers
substitute a picture of a red heart for the word love and apply it to just about anything,
anybody, or any place. In some Christian gatherings people are asked to turn around and
look the person next to them full in the face, even if he is a perfect stranger, and say with
a broad smile and without the least trace of a blush, "God loves you, and so do I."[1]
—ELISABETH ELLIOT

It's easy to see why so many are asking, "What's love got to do with God?" Love has been neutralized, watered down, and cheapened by our culture. Yet, love has everything to do with God. Why would want to water down the power and truth of something so real and beautiful and toss it aside? Perh. because it doesn't seem real or practical enough for our everyday realities.

Let me tell you something—Jesus Christ is the most practical and personal everyday reality y will ever come to know. God the Father sent His Son, Jesus, in a "real" form—the reality of flesh— us to see, follow, and believe in. His testimony has lasted throughout the ages. The realness of Je Christ was God in the flesh for our ultimate salvation and deliverance. Our God is not only migh full of wisdom and strength, but He is also real and at work in the real things that fill up our live

God is the great conductor of our lives. He is orchestrating each note in the music of our perso journey. At this very moment, God is at work. The tragedy is that we have a deep longing to know G and experience His love, yet we are unable to recognize Him and His love even though He embraces in His love day after day. Far too often we attribute God's work to circumstance or coincidence rat than admitting that God is fitting all the pieces of our lives together.

Take a puzzle and empty out the box. Look at all those little pieces with various shapes, sizes, a colors. To me the puzzle just looks like a heap of pieces, a mess to untangle. That is how the pie of our lives sometimes look to us. They don't seem to make sense. Sometimes we come upon a m shapen and discolored piece. We can't imagine how this ugly piece can fit into the picture. Yet we m remember that God's ways are not our ways. His ways are higher and always right. He is putting picture together. He is placing the high notes and the low notes in harmonizing order. He is alw working according to plan—His plan.

 DAY ONE: HE COMPLETES ME

1. Write out Psalm 138:8.

• According to this verse, what will the Lord do for you?

Look up the word *fulfill* and write down the definition.

What does "the LORD will fulfill his purpose for me" mean to you?

I am encouraged that God carries out His plans for my life. I find this is personal and enables me to trust Him in tangible ways. This truth makes me secure. When my personal life was splintered and shattered, I held on to this verse. It was my promise. Despite what I could see, God was fulfilling His purposes for me. Despite the ugly, misshapen pieces I was handed, God was never going to abandon the work of His hand—me.

Now as my children are grown, I find amazing comfort in knowing that God will fulfill His purpose for them. As much as I love my children, God loves them more. He will not abandon the works of His hands. What hope and joy this brings to me. I can apply this to my life every day in real and practical ways! I can encourage my son with the Scriptures and pass on to him truth to embrace, truth to find hope in, and a solid foundation on which to trust.

. **Read the following verses, and summarize how each relationship with the Lord was practical and personal. What do you see in these interactions with God that can be applied to your own life, though your circumstances are different?**
Adam and Eve: Genesis 3:20–21
Summary:

Application:

Hagar: Genesis 16:1–13
Summary:

Application:

• Solomon: 1 Kings 3:5–13
Summary:

Application:

3. Read the following verses. Summarize how each person experienced God's deliverance, powe
   and authority. (Be sure to notice God's obvious care about practicality and details.)
• The disciples: Mark 6:7–13

• Paul: 2 Corinthians 12:7–10

• Peter: Acts 12:1–17

• John: Revelation 1:9–20

4. Read Hebrews 13:8. What does this verse say to you about Jesus Christ?

Lord,
If I stop and look, I can see Your hand all around me. Cause me to stop and
look today. Amen.

 DAY TWO: DO NOT WORRY ABOUT YOUR LIFE

**Read Matthew 6:25–34. How do these verses show that Jesus was practical in His dealings
with people?**

Rewrite the passage, personalizing it in your own words.

According to Matthew 6:25–34, what practical things are you not to worry about?

What does Jesus say about you in Matthew 6:26?

I encourage you to believe the truth that you are valuable to God!

What does Matthew 6:28–32 say to you about the practical and personal side of God?

• In Matthew 6:31–32, what does your heavenly Father know?

Can you grasp with me that the God of the universe, the Alpha and Omega, the Creator of all thir knows us in such a personal way that He knows what is necessary, useful, and desirable in our lives?

God certainly knew how to reassure and help Moses. In Exodus 3:11 we read that Moses could understand why God would choose someone like him. He said to God, "Who am I, that I should to Pharaoh and bring the Israelites out of Egypt?" God answered him with the practical truth of t situation: "I will be with you" (Ex. 3:12).

Need:

—something necessary

—something useful

—something desirable

Moses, still trying to comprehend what was happening, ask God, "Suppose I go to the Israelites and say to them, 'The G of your fathers has sent me to you,' and they ask me, 'What is name?' Then what shall I tell them?" (Ex. 3:13).

God answered Moses simply, "I AM WHO I AM" (Ex. 3:14).

God's name, I AM, says much about the realness and practical side of God. In that name is ever thing that we will ever need. He is the answer to our problems, the healer of our hearts, the joy of o souls, the designer of our lives. He is who He said He is, and He will be with us. This is not only re it is practical.

You wouldn't think of sending children out into the dark, cold night alone. This would not be practical thing to do. The wise and practical thing would be to send someone with them—someone strong, wise, and safe. Like the loving Father He is, God has not sent us out alone. He is with us alwa Jesus told His disciples before His death, "I will not leave you as orphans; I will come to you. Befc long, the world will not see me anymore, but you will see me. Because I live, you also will live. On th day you will *realize* that I am in my Father, and you are in me, and I am in you" (John 14:18–20).

God knows everything we need, and He can provide it for us. If we don't have something, we mu not really need it at this time. He is in us. He works within us. And He is "I AM" to each of us.

2. Read Matthew 6:5–8. What do these verses say about God knowing you, especially His pra
   tical involvement in your life?

The most practical thing you can do is to have a God-centered life. From this position you can experience God's love on a daily basis. This is contrary to the wisdom of the world. The Bible focuses on God, while much of the self-help material on the market focuses on self. You have a choice. You must decide whether you will live a God-centered life or a self-centered life. The whole concept behind salvation is dying to self. In order to know and experience God's love, we must deny self and develop a God-centered heart.

Lord,
I thank You that Your love for me covers all. You care for me and love me beyond what I could humanly comprehend. Your love is all I need to count on throughout my life. Help me to recognize and remember this. Amen.

 DAY THREE: HOLDING FAST TO CHRIST

Read Deuteronomy 30:19–20. Record your thoughts of how the following directives relate to you personally. Why should we follow them?
choose life

love the LORD your God

listen to his voice

hold fast to him

But … what if you blow it? Write out the following verses.
John 1:9

Acts 10:43

Ephesians 1:7

Redemption is when someone redeems something, buying it back or recovering it. Do you need be redeemed? Do you need to be recovered from past sins, present fears, and future anxieties? Well good and practical news! Because of God's love, the blood of Jesus Christ has redeemed you. His bloo purchased you—bought you back—so that you would be His forever.

3. Write out Psalm 130:7–8. Substitute your name for the name Israel.

4. Write out Colossians 1:14.

Do you need forgiveness today? Forgiveness is a real and practical aspect of God's love. Each day is important that we ask God to cleanse us from all sin and anything that would get in the way of o relationship with Him. Jesus Christ has paved the w for forgiveness. We shouldn't think of forgiveness or in terms of the biggies—the big sins—rather we shou think of forgiveness in terms of all of our "stuff." I ha never met a woman without "stuff." So fess up and cleansed by the blood of Jesus. His forgiveness is awesome and wonderful grace that does the mirac lous work of an eraser on the sin in our lives.

I know that my Redeemer lives, and that in the end he will stand upon the earth. And after my skin has been destroyed, yet in my flesh I will see God; I myself will see him with my own eyes—I, and not another. How my heart yearns within me! (Job 19:25–27)

Write out Philippians 2:13.

According to Philippians 2:13, who is working in you?

What is the purpose of His working?

If you stay Christ-centered, you will be allowing God to work actively in you. When you see things ppen around you, you will become excited about what He is doing in and through you. You will perience Him working in your life in the most practical of ways.

Dear Father,
When I am focused on the truth of Your Word I am lined up to a pipeline of encouragement. To think that You, the Lord God Almighty, are at work in little ol' me is a thought beyond any blessing I could ever ask for. But it's true. You are working in me, I am Yours, and by Your work in an everyday life, may You be glorified. Amen.

 DAY FOUR: THE ABCs

Step A: Start out the day choosing God.

1. **Read Deuteronomy 30:19–20. What do you think it means in practice to "choose life"?**

• What else does this passage say about choosing God?

2. **Read Joshua 24:15. What is a practical way in which you could choose to serve God ahead other gods?**

3. **Read Matthew 6:33. What does seeking God's kingdom first involve?**

Step B: Listen to God's voice.

4. **Read John 10:2–5. How can you distinguish God's voice from the other voices that comp for your attention?**

5. **Read John 14:17. Are you aware of the Spirit living in you? Talk about your awareness or la of it.**

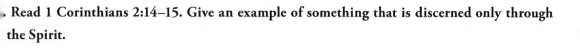

Read 1 Corinthians 2:14–15. Give an example of something that is discerned only through the Spirit.

Read Ephesians 6:17. How can the Word of God be the Spirit's sword in your life?

he real change happens with Step C: Love God through obedience.

Read John 14:15, 24. Why is obedience to God a necessary response to love for God?

Read John 15:10. In order to remain (dwell, live) in His love, Jesus says we have to obey His commands. Have we shifted here from relationship to rule-keeping? Why, or why not?

Father,
May I seek Your face, Your kingdom, and Your will above all else. May I learn to say *yes* to You even when I want to say *no*—knowing that You are my Father and You love me. Your way is always right. Amen.

DAY FIVE: CONFIDENCE IN GOD

1. Read Hebrews 10:35–39.

• What does *persevere* mean?

• What ways of persevering does this passage describe?

• Why is it so important not to give up trusting God's love?

• Are you tempted to give up? If so, what tempts you?

2. Read Hebrews 11:6. Why is faith (trust) in God so important?

The LORD
Almighty
is with us
(Ps. 46:7).

**3. Read Hebrews 12:1–3. What motivations to trust God and keep going c
you find in this passage?**

How can you fix your eyes on Jesus today? What helps, and what hinders?

Write out Joshua 24:23–24.

> God's love meets us where the rubber meets the road in our lives. This kind of love is real and practical!

Is any of this real and practical to you? Allowing God to become a practical part of your everyday is what the Bible and biblical principles are all about. Too many times we pick and choose what want to obey and believe, thus developing our own brand of "relationship." We then wonder why we l no different about life than our unbelieving friends. A woman who is walking with God should different. I'm not talking about a difference that is measured by a set of good works. I'm talking out a difference that is regulated in her heart. Who is she? What does she stand for? Is her God real, is He just a God of nice thoughts and flowery proposals?

God is real, powerful, practical. Ask Him by the power of His Holy Spirit to show you the lity of His presence in your everyday life this week. Be prepared share something practical, powerful, or real that God has done in y area of your life.

> In all your ways acknowledge him, and he will make your paths straight (Prov. 3:6).

When Mother Teresa received her Nobel Prize, someone asked r, "What can we do to promote world peace?" She replied, "Go me and love your family."

> *Get Christ Himself in the focus of your heart and keep Him there continually. Only in Christ will you find complete fulfillment. Throw your heart open to the Holy Spirit and invite Him to fill you. He will do it. Let no one interpret the Scriptures for you in such a way as to rule out the Father's gift of the Spirit. Every man is as full of the Spirit as he wants to be. Make your heart a vacuum and the Spirit will rush in to fill it.[2]*
>
> —A. W. Tozer

Dear Lord,

Come and fill me with Yourself, make me completely Yours. Anoint me each day for that day's steps. Guide me … step by step … in this journey of life. May I always see You, look for You in everything and everyone. I desire to be Your vessel and a woman whom You can use, by the power of the Spirit of God at work within me. Thank You for redeeming me, and now I will trust in You, my Redeemer who lives! Amen.

Journal Page

God moves us practically, doesn't He? He told Moses to go and lead the children of Israel; He told Noah to build an ark; He told Paul to trust in the strength of God. What is He telling you to do today?

_____

_____

_____

_____

_____

_____

_____

_____

_____

_____

_____

_____

_____

_____

_____

_____

_____

_____

_____

KEY POINTS FROM LESSON 3

- God is with me.
- He perfects all that concerns me.
- He accomplishes His will in me.
- He works in practical ways—using my "regular" life as a lesson for the journey.
- He is always with me, ever faithful.
- He knows all that I need and is my provision.
- Because He loves me I do not need to worry about my provisions.
- My part is to choose life in Christ.
- I am to hold fast to God through my relationship with His Son, Jesus.
- The Spirit of God is at work in and through me—for God's good pleasure.
- I must return to elementary living and practice the basics:

  A—Start my day choosing God.

  B—Listen to His voice each day.

  C—Love Him through obedience.
- When I come near to God, He too draws near to me.

Love Created Me

*All of God's people are ordinary people who have been made
extraordinary by the purpose He has given them.*

—OSWALD CHAMBERS

All things were created by him and for him.

—COLOSSIANS 1:16

s easy to forget where our true roots are. "In the beginning God created...." Many of us grew up
ating our beginnings to two love-struck people we learned to call our parents. Some of us grew
relating our beginnings to a mistake or an accident by two people who didn't really welcome our
rival into the world. We have forgotten that even though it takes two people to perform the physical
t that can lead to a pregnancy, only God can create the miracle of life within the womb. God does
t create mistakes. Your life is a miracle of God's design.

I know only too well how hard it can be to conceive a child. Longing to be a mother, I was one of
ose temperature-taking, month-charting women, who spent a few years desperately trying to plan
timacy at the exact right time. I wanted so much to become pregnant and have a child that I bought
e books and kits and followed all the timeline rules.

Originally I assumed it would be easy. You just get pregnant, right? Wrong! Though we did all the
oper things according to the latest fertility books, I was not conceiving. Finally, after what seemed
ke forever, in what I now know was God's perfect timing, I conceived my first child. Even though
e were doing all the "right" things, the element missing was God's perfect timing for His plan to be

completed and His child to be born. Life is not an accident! It is ordained by God. Try as I might,
could not make pregnancy happen one day earlier than planned by God.

Like most women I experience great joy when I see little babies. I *ooh* and *ahh* over each intricate
feature from head to toe. A new life has such promise. A new life is like a clean slate, a new beginning,
something new and beautiful entering the world. Once this new little person enters the scene, nothing
will ever be exactly as it was before.

So it is with you! Once you entered the scene nothing was ever the same again! You were the one
that people *oohed* and *aahed* over. They scrutinized all your little features to see just whom you looked
like, and they saw all the promise of tomorrow in your birth. (And if they didn't, that wasn't because
of something lacking in you.)

It's easy for us to recognize the promise and miracle of life in a newborn, but what about stopping
right now to recognize the promise and miracle of your life? Rejoice in the day God created you!

 DAY ONE: FEARFULLY AND WONDERFULLY MADE

**1. Read Psalm 139:1–17. Underline the verses that speak to your heart about your beginning.
Write out your favorite verse.**

• Fill in the following:

My birth name _____

Date of birth _____

2. Write out Psalm 139:13.

According to Psalm 139:13, who created you? Why does that matter?

What was happening in your mother's womb?

Look up the definition of *knit* and write it here.

Write out Psalm 119:73.

According to Psalm 119:73, whose hands formed you? What goes on inside you when you think about that?

Lord,
I often forget the miracle of my birth, my existence, my part in Your plan. Help me to go deeper than surface things and realize the importance of creation, especially You creating me for Your purposes. Thank You for life. Amen.

 DAY TWO: MADE IN HIS IMAGE

1. Write out Genesis 1:27.

• In what ways are you made in God's image?

• How do you usually view yourself?

• How does viewing yourself negatively affect your feelings and actions?

The way some of us view ourselves is a problem today. Not many women feel good about them selves. And given the media pressure of our culture, it is no wonder we struggle with our image of ourselves. Images of women who are flawless according to the world's standard are all around us.

Even though we are Christians, we still tend to measure ourselves against the images before us Measuring ourselves with the world's standard is like measuring ourselves with a broken ruler—we will never get an accurate measurement. We will always be lacking because the tool with which we measured ourselves is inaccurate. But when we measure ourselves with the ruler of God's Word, we measure ourselves accurately every time. Unfortunately, even Christian women fail to look to God's measuring system for the foundation of security for which we long.

It is easy to get caught up in feeling worthless. It is not uncommon for us to feel as if we a bodies when we fail to achieve in some area. When we feel worthless, we act worthless. Instead faith ruling our lives, insecurity rules our thoughts and actions. We perceive ourselves a certain y, and then we act out those perceptions. Some call this living by a perceived identity. Clearly, our tions, attitudes, choices, and responses to life are all affected by how we view ourselves. Sadly, since ost of us have an inaccurate and unbiblical view of ourselves, we act out in ways that are contrary to od's design for us.

The answer to this dilemma is seeing ourselves as God's loved and accepted children. When we e ourselves as God's children, we will live as His. When we perceive our life as valuable, we will live cording to that value system. We need to ask God to change our perceived identity and give us our e identity, according to His Word.

Read Genesis 2:7. According to this verse, who gave you your first breath?

Why does that matter?

How easy it is for us to think of a baby's first breath as just a response to the doctor's spank on the by's bottom. The child comes out, the doctor clears the nasal passages, holds the child upside down, d then with a little pat, out comes the bellowing cry of the newborn. Babies are born every day. The rthing procedures have become commonplace.

In the fast pace of life, sometimes we take for granted the miracles of life. Maybe you weren't mpted to take all the details of your own child's, or loved one's, birth for granted, but what about ur life, your birth? What about the fact that God breathed into you the breath of life and you came a living person? Does that mean anything to you?

Most of us take for granted that we are alive. But we must remember that life is a gift and it is luable to God. Our lives have purpose and value and will continue to have purpose and value until e allows the breath of life to cease.

What would be a God-centered response to all of this?

3. Write out Psalm 139:14.

• What are the two words used in Psalm 139:14 to describe how you were made?

• What is the word used in this verse to describe God's works?

• What is the psalmist's point about you?

Unfortunately, not many women know full well that they are a wonderful work of God's han If we did know that, we would live differently. We would feel different about ourselves, our futur and our lives. Sadly, we get trapped in the same way unbelievers might get trapped—in our pasts, our inadequacies, and especially in looking only at appearances and achievements. These are some the things that drag us down and keep us from experiencing God the way we would like to. We m definitely need to have our minds renewed!

4. Read Isaiah 46:3–4. How long has God held you?

• How long will He continue to carry you?

Who sustains your life?

What else does He do?

Lord,

Please forgive me for not realizing that I was made in Your image. Instead I put myself down, doubt if I have any value, and spend countless hours wasted on negative self-focus. I no longer want to be that kind of woman. Instead create in me a heart that remembers who she is and whose she is, so that my time is focused on the magnitude of Your plan and a life that was created to live for You. Amen.

  DAY THREE: PRESENT YOURSELF TO GOD

Write out Romans 12:1–2.

According to Romans 12:1–2, why should you present your life to God?

Read Colossians 1:16.

- According to this verse, you (and everything else) were created "in him"—that is, in Christ. Wh does that mean?

- You were also created "by him and for him." What does that mean?

- What are the implications for the way you view yourself and conduct your life?

- Do you think it's reasonable for God to want you to submit your life to Him as you are instructed in Romans 12:1? Why or why not?

3. Look up the following words in a dictionary. Write the meanings here.
transform

renew

- How do these descriptions give you a picture of what can happen to you when your mind is renewe in the truths of God's Word?

Some of us have had a negative or less-than-God-inspired pattern of thinking built into us over ᵉ years. This patterning may affect several areas. The foundational issue we need to address in this ɪrney of learning God's love is how we view ourselves. Negative thoughts and self-defeating patterns ᵉ contrary to the knowledge of God.

ɪnstead of being fashioned after the world and its patterns, for what are you supposed to reach?

Lord,
I am seeing that I have become accustomed to the world I live in and the view of me according to this present culture. I no longer want to be inspired or discouraged by a culture that is mainly material and not eternity focused. I want to line up to what Your Word says is truth. To do this I need to have my mind renewed. Show me the way to live in this renewal. Amen.

 DAY FOUR: BRINGING MY MIND TO CHRIST

Write out 2 Corinthians 10:5.

What does this verse tell you to do with your thoughts?

How does a person do this?

• What are some of the thoughts you have struggled with about yourself?

The Bible gives us the truth by which to pattern our thinking. When we become saturated with t new way of thinking, we will have a new way of life as well. The power of the Bible is not just in rea

ing it or memorizing the words. The pov of the Bible comes when we begin to thi biblical thoughts. That's what meditating the Word is all about—not just reading a memorizing, but reflecting, thinking, che ing on the words as if they were our o personal message from God. After all, t *truly are our personal message from God!*

Ralph Waldo Emerson said, "A man is what he thinks about all day long." Marcus Aurelius said, "A man's life is what his thoughts make it." Norman Vincent Peale said, "Change your thoughts and you change your world." The Bible says, "For as he thinketh in his heart, so is he" (Prov. 23:7 KJV).

I like to think of studying the Bible as marinating in the truth. I soak in it, letting it flavor w I am, season who I become, tenderize all the tough spots in my heart. I don't have to understa everything about God's Word in order for it to work on my life; I just have to know that it does wo it does change me from the inside out.

2. Read 2 Timothy 3:16. What does this verse say to you about God's Word?

3. Write out Hebrews 4:12.

Wow, the Word of God goes deep, doesn't it? It goes so deep that it can expose the thoughts a titudes of our hearts. We all need that kind of probing and realigning. Next time you feel a negative tack coming on, hold up what you are thinking about yourself to the Word of Truth. How does it compare? What is real and true, no matter what you see or feel?

Write out Revelation 4:11.

Everybody suffers when we don't realize our personal worth. *We suffer.* We aren't free to express our love, uniqueness, and fts. *Others suffer.* The way we feel about ourselves affects the ay we relate to others.

> Accepting the fact that you are loved and valuable is essential. Be transformed by the renewing of your mind!

Father,
I grew up with dreams of what I could be, with not much thought of what You created me for. I had these thoughts because I didn't know any different. But now I am learning truth, and the truth is that I was created for Your pleasure. This is exciting. I wonder what You have for me? What will please You to do through me? Oh, Father, make me completely Yours! Amen.

DAY FIVE: THE REALITY OF GOD'S LOVE FOR ME

Read Psalm 139 again. This time read it out loud, slowly and deliberately. Let God's thoughts toward you and His involvement in your life sink in a little deeper.
Now write out every *fact* you find in Psalm 139 that expresses God's knowledge of you or His love for you.

2. Read Ephesians 4:29–30. What do these verses say about your self-talk and how you p
yourself down?

> *A healthy, positive self-esteem is not attained by "feel good" superficiality. On the other*
> *hand, a Christ-centered view of ourselves is not detrimental to true discipleship; it is*
> *the result of understanding and applying the truths of the Scriptures. A proper view of*
> *God and of ourselves enables us to love, obey, and honor Christ with full hearts.*[1]
>
> —ROBERT MCGEE

3. Write out Philippians 1:6.

God created you. He created you in love because He values you. Everything God creates is goc and for a purpose (1 Tim. 4:4). Therefore, you don't have compare yourself with others ever again. Each woman unique. God's plan for each of us is different. He isn't ma ing cookie-cutter Christians—it's our immaturity th produces copycat people. Each one of us has a part in Goc plan. His plan is to conform us more into His image ar draw us closer to Himself. We make it so hard, but He did make it as complex as we do. He told us to believe in Hir

> Though outwardly we are wasting away, yet inwardly we are being renewed day by day.... So we fix our eyes not on what is seen, but on what is unseen. For what is seen is temporary, but what is unseen is eternal (2 Cor. 4:16, 18).

love Him, abide in Him, and love others. Let us do just that!

- Believe God is intimately concerned with you, your soul, and your eternal future.
- Love God as a response to understanding His great love for you.
- Abide in Him, connecting to Him each morning for power and strength.
- Love others, for they too were created in the image of God, for His purposes.

Jewels in the Lord's Crown

Women are precious jewels to the Lord.
Some of us are sapphires bold and brilliant,
filled with the power of God's love.
While some are rubies filled with the energy and enthusiasm,
to share God's love.
Others are topaz, warm and merciful
in their commitment to those lives they touch for God.
Those who are amethyst are quiet and gentle,
lifting the people they meet in prayer.
And others are diamonds, strong and powerful
in their desire to draw the unsaved to the Lord.
As we intertwine to form a crown to lay before the Lord,
He rejoices not in the brilliance or the value of the jewels,
but in the love that binds our hearts together.

—DONNA BURKE

Choose the verse of Scripture that meant the most to you this week and write it on an index card. Carry it with you each day this week. Read it often as you strive to think God's thoughts.

Go through your old pictures and find a childhood photo of urself. Share this picture with the women in your fellowship oup. If you aren't doing this study with other women, then just get e picture out for yourself. Reflect on who God created when He t you together in your mother's womb. Look at the picture several nes this week. Perhaps you can even use it, for just this week, as ookmark in your Bible. Each time you look at that picture, tell urself, *"God created me!"*

Know therefore that the LORD your God is God; he is the faithful God, keeping his covenant of love to a thousand generations of those who love him and keep his commands (Deut. 7:9).

Dear Lord,

Forgive me for all the times I have taken life for granted. You have given me life and breath. I have neglected to thank You for who I am and who You are faithfully forming me to be. I look at the negative, You dwell on the positive. I look at impossible, You look at possibilities. I want more than anything to be renewed in my mind and changed in my thinking. Make this a reality in my life, as I marinate in Your Word, soaking in all that is true about me ... in You. Amen.

Journal Page

This week I have noticed truths differently. The ones that stand out as a Technicolor reality are …

KEY POINTS FROM LESSON 4

- I have been created by God—in His image.
- I have been created for God—He has a plan.
- I have been made by the Master—wonderful are His works.
- From birth He has held me.
- Even unto my gray hairs He will keep me.
- Forever I will be with Him.
- I am breathing today because of Him, alive by design.
- I am to present this gift of my life to Him.
- I am to no longer be conformed to the world, but renewed to live for Christ.
- I suffer if I don't hold on to the truth of who I am in Christ and whose I am as His.
- He is intimately concerned about me in every aspect of my life.

Love Ordains My Days

*If you are going to be used by God, He will take you through a
number of experiences that are not meant for you personally at
all. They are designed to make you useful in His hands.*

—OSWALD CHAMBERS

All the days ordained for me were written in your book before one of them came to be.

—PSALM 139:16

emember wondering what I would be when I grew up. Thoughts of the perfect life filled my mind

a young age, and unrealistic expectations shaped my dreams of the future. On occasion my mother

ng this song to me:

*When I was just a little girl,
I asked my mother what would I be
Will I be pretty? Will I be rich?
Here's what she said to me.
"Que Sera Sera, Whatever will be, will be
The future's not ours to see
Que Sera Sera."*

Here I am today, grown up and still wondering at times, *"Lord, what am I going to be?"* or more

curately, *"Lord, who am I, and where am I going?"* We all would like to know the future, or at least we think we would like to know it. I take great comfort in knowing that God has planned my days—the length of them and the breadth of them. This security has changed me.

 DAY ONE: ORDAINED FOR GOD'S PURPOSES

1. Write out Psalm 139:16.

This is one of my favorite verses. It gives me great confidence and peace. When this truth sinks deep within my very soul, I can then have a new perspective of my life and be more patient with the overall plan—the big picture. When God corrects me, deals with me, or allows things to cross my path, I have the hope that He knows exactly what shape my life is supposed to take and that He will be the faithful power at work within me to mold me into the woman He has designed me to be.

> He has ordained my days.
> Ordain: to set forth expressly and with authority, to dictate, to put in order, to establish by appointment, to prescribe, to call the shots, to tune, to lay it on the line.

Notice here that Psalm 139:16 doesn't say *some* of my days, but *all* my days. Have you had days that didn't add up in your mind to the love of God?

I don't know about you, but sometimes something small as a bad hair day can really set me off. That is, until I get a grip and begin praising God in the midst of everything every day, always! Life is not always a joy ride. Some seasons are very hard. That is why we need the hope of knowing that our life is in His hand … always has been, always will be.

> *Wherever we find ourselves, God has a reason for placing us there. He has His hand upon our lives and upon each circumstance in our lives. We may be going through difficult trials, but hardships are necessary. God wants to develop in us the characteristics that will enable us to fulfill His plan for us. God is working in each of us.*[1]
> —CHUCK SMITH

How exciting to realize that God is putting my life in order. He is setting up divine appointments that bring forth His will in my life. He is calling the shots and fine-tuning each part of me for His ory. And it is all happening through circumstances He has planned for me to encounter.

Write out 1 Peter 2:9.

What do these statements about you mean?

For what do you think you are chosen?

Write out Ephesians 2:10.

The Greek word for workmanship is *poiema*. This word means "masterpiece, work of art, poem." he bottom line is this: You are His work, His poetry, His expression, His masterpiece. This is the uth about you. God will work in you by His grace and power so that He might accomplish the plan e has for you, for His kingdom and His glory.

What is the result of being chosen by God?

82

Lord,

Open my eyes to see the beauty of Your handiwork in creating us. May I no longer refute how You made me, but instead embrace Your plan, Your creation, Your handiwork as the truth of what it is—the truth of what I am—a wonderful work of God. Amen.

 DAY TWO: BY HIM AND FOR HIM

1. Write out Colossians 1:16. (We studied this before, but our practice is to review passages aga to let them sink in.)

By Him and for Him. Those few words now give new meaning to my life. They are my person slogan. They explain what I live for and who I live for. My unspoken slogan used to be *by me and f me.* Everything was always just about me. What does Debbie want? But those words—*by Him a for Him*—simplify my purpose and meaning. They simplify my choices and help me focus on wha important.

• How will *by Him and for Him* affect the way you live today?

2. Write out Jeremiah 1:5.

• Do you think God knows and sets apart only special people like Jeremiah? What makes you think tha

What if someone said, "But my life is so ordinary. I've never done anything great, and I've made so many mistakes." Are those good reasons for a person to think that she doesn't count for much in God's eyes? Why, or why not?

God created you for His purposes! Before you were born, He set you apart. Think about that. Next time you are tempted to think your life doesn't have any purpose—don't go there! Instead, go to the Word of God and drink in the truth of His purpose—by Him and for Him.

God has set us apart for His purposes. He knows what He intends to do, and He knows the proper activity that suits us expressly, according to His design of who we are as individuals. Knowing that He has ordained our days gives us purpose and meaning. Knowing that He planned for us gives us vision for the future and for all that He has intended for us.

You Dreamed Me Up

O dear God, it was You, You alone who dreamed me up.
Nobody else would ever have thought of me
or planned for me,
or looked right through me with future contemplation.
Right from the beginning of time I was all Your idea.
You had big things in mind for me, good things,
glorious things.
And now, with magnificent dexterity You are making
them come to pass.
And I! Well, I stand amazed on the sideline and praise
Your infinite patience. [2]

—RUTH HARMS CALKIN

Father,

I look to You, the Master Planner of all things great and small. I look to You the Author and Finisher of my faith, my life, and my future. Today I look to You. Amen.

 DAY THREE: RESTORATION 101

1. Read Matthew 4:19 and 28:18–20.

• According to these verses, what is one of the purposes in the life of Jesus' disciples?

• Does this apply to you? Why, or why not?

God is determined to save the lost and restore lives. God created each of us to share in this p pose. Within each of us are genetics and characteristics that make us unique women. God loves us a calls us His "wonderful work." He takes joy in using us for His glory. His desire for our lives is that would bring praise, glory, and honor to Him.

Do you have to be an evangelist, leading thousands to Jesus, to bring glory to God? No. You ne to be you. If part of being you is evangelizing large groups, then *go for it*. But if being you is servi meals to the needy, then serve them with all your heart. If being you is helping someone decorate home, adding beauty and peace to her environment, then do it with flair and joy!

Whatever you do, do that very thing unto the Lord, whether it is changing diapers, driving c pools, running corporate meetings, cooking for your family, being there for your friends, or shari the gospel. Do all for the glory of God!

2. Read Luke 19:10. What was Jesus' goal in coming to this earth?

What does this have to do with you?

God wants to bring people to a love relationship with Jesus Christ. A relationship where we remain Him, renew ourselves in Him, and rest in Him. As we understand that His love involves using us in the circumstances we find ourselves in, we get excited about being used by God.

God is making us into everyday vessels through which He can pour Himself each day. Unlike fragile china teapot, we will become strong and durable. A special little pot that requires special andling only gets taken off the shelf for special occasions—not so for the strong and durable everyday ssel. We are being made strong, secure, and durable for God's purposes each day. This happens as we t into the Word of God and learn more about who God is and what His plan is.

Don't wait for a special occasion to be open to God's use. Start today. Remember that He has plans at are being carried out right this moment.

Read Romans 8:28–30. Think about these verses and jot down your responses to the facts below.

od works for the good in all things

am called according to His purpose

od foreknew me. (He called me from my mother's womb.)

od predestined me to be conformed to the likeness of His Son (changed from the inside out)

od called me

God justified me (set me into a right relationship with Himself despite my sin)

God glorified me

> *It is only a faithful person who truly believes that God sovereignly controls his circumstances. We take our circumstances for granted, saying God is in control, but not really believing it. We act as if the things that happen were completely controlled by people. To be faithful in every circumstance means that we have only one loyalty, or object of our faith—the Lord Jesus Christ. God may cause our circumstances to suddenly fall apart, which may bring the realization of our unfaithfulness to Him for not recognizing that He had ordained the situation. We never saw what He was trying to accomplish, and that exact event will never be repeated in our life. This is where the test of our faithfulness comes. If we will just learn to worship God even during the difficult circumstances, He will change them for the better very quickly if He so chooses.[3]*
>
> —OSWALD CHAMBERS

4. Read Romans 8:31–39. According to these verses, what reasons for confidence do you have?

• What can separate you from the love of Christ?

• Why is that important?

Romans 8 is incredibly powerful. Read it over and over again. Let it sink into your thoughts, ckle down into your heart, and change your perspective.

Knowing that God created you, chose you, and has your days mapped out can give you a nderful new perspective. It is exciting to think that God is in control. Even control freaks can rn to take comfort in the fact that God is in charge, and nothing can separate you from Him d His love for you.

His love for us is the motivating factor in all : does. Love is who He is. Love is His nature. We n have victory in our hardships and our triumphs cause of the love of God. Paul says we are more than nquerors through Him who loved us.

> It's trendy to get yourself together and get on a spiritual path. A spiritual path to where? It is all vague and uncertain. Get spiritual, be the best you can be, you only have one life to live.

Don't yawn! Don't fall asleep! Don't just think *here go with that love stuff again.* Over and over we read of God's love. Yet over and over again we take 'or granted and don't acknowledge that it is a powerful force in our lives, ordaining our days and 'ing us purpose. Embracing His steadfast love can change your life. It is changing mine daily!

Father,
On one hand Your love seems so simplistic and on the other it is so hard to understand. I want to be enthralled with Your love, basking in it daily, resting in it, nesting in it—and experiencing life change as a result of it. Amen.

Day Four: For Such a Time as This

Read Romans 9:16. On what does God's choice of family members depend?

s it influenced by your efforts? Why is this important?

2. Read Esther 4:12–14.

God raised Esther up to become a king's wife so that at the proper time she could have an influence sparing the Jewish people. When she found out about a plot to have the Jewish people wiped out, Esther to persuade her husband to stop it. But it was dangerous for her to take action because her husband co likely have killed her along with the other Jews. That's why her uncle Mordecai sent this message to her.

• If Esther did nothing, because of feeling helpless or afraid, what did Mordecai think would happe

• What if Esther thought, *God is so powerful, He can handle this without me?* What would have be wrong with thinking like this?

• When you think about God ordaining you for a specific time and purpose, what goes throu your mind?

3. Write out Psalm 4:3.

4. Read Psalm 20.

Often we don't understand the purpose of situations we face. In these times especially we sho put all our trust in the Lord our God. We need to ask for His direction and praise Him that He everything in His hand. By His power He will move into our lives.

Write out Psalm 21:7. Personalize this verse by putting your name in the place of the word *king.*

It is a wonderful trait to be secure and not shaken. We can be! We can be so confident in God and the *fact* that He is a sovereign God always working the purposes of His will in us that we are not shaken by any circumstance.

Lord,
Because of You I will not be shaken. Work in me a sincere authentic trust, that I might declare, "I trust in the unfailing love of the Most High." Amen.

 DAY FIVE: HE VALUES THOSE HE HAS MADE

Write out Psalm 22:5.

Write out Psalm 22:9–10.

What is the Lord trying to say to you through this psalm?

Read Psalm 139:17–18 again.

God's thoughts toward us are more in number than the grains of sand. Have you ever tri∉ counting sand? I tried it one day. It was impossible. To me this is a beautiful picture of ho⋯

> The Lord will perfect that which concerns me; Your mercy and loving-kindness, O Lord, endure forever—forsake not the works of Your own hands (Ps. 138:8 AB).

impossible it is to count God's thoughts about me. He h⋯ plans, He has intentions, and He is always thinking of m⋯ Thank God that it is He who fashioned my days! Next tir⋯ you are with your child, grandchild, or friend at the park⋯ beach, pick up a handful of sand. Let it slip through yo⋯ fingers and see for yourself.

3. For each of these proverbs, write down how its teaching is relevant to you.
Proverbs 19:21

Proverbs 19:22

Proverbs 20:24

Proverbs 21:30

> Many are the plans in a [woman's] heart, but it is the LORD's purpose that prevails. What a [woman] desires is unfailing love (Prov. 19:21–22).

God ordains compassion and love toward me.

I wrote a song for a friend of mine in 1980. When ⋯ were young adults, she was my very first friend to ha⋯ a baby, and when I saw her beautiful new daughter, t⋯ reality of the magnificent miracle of God's creative wo⋯ swept over me.

I was completely taken by the miracle of life. The realization that God planned this little gi⋯ Micah, became very real to me. As I thanked God for Micah's birth, I wrote this song. It lat⋯ became my own sons' song as I often sang these same words that were originally written for Mic⋯

uers to Justin and Cameron. In many ways it is a song for us all, because nothing could have
pped our birth. We are alive as a result of God's plan.

Micah's Song

Little baby, born today
Nothing could have stood in the way
For you are a part of God's plan.
Precious one, so soft and sweet
I hope we can teach you to sit at the feet
Of Jesus. He has a purpose just for you.
As we look at you now, child,
We must believe you are part of a plan
Designed by God's own hand.
His special, our special, little one.

Keep in your mind the truth that you were created by God—for Him.

By Him and for Him! You are part of His plan—just believe it. He has a plan carved out just
· you. Stick close to His side, so you don't miss a beat!

Remember the baby or childhood picture I asked you to take out? Have you been using it for
ookmark, or has it been in clear view this week? Well, guess what? I took out a picture of myself
p. It is an old black-and-white photo of a four-year-old girl on top of a little pony, with a huge
ut on her face. I put it in a frame that says, "Bloom where you are planted." I placed it out with

the other family pictures to remind me that not only
s I created by God, but I am to let my roots go down
ep into Him regardless of my circumstances. For surely,
all things He is at work conforming me into His image.
at is what He has ordained, set forth, prescribed,
pointed for me, His child.

I will cry to God Most High,
Who performs on my behalf and
rewards me [Who brings to pass
His purposes for me and surely
completes them!] (Ps. 57:2 AB).

Dear Lord,

May I never take my life for granted. You had something in mind when You created me. You are working in me even now, molding me and shaping me, conforming me into Your image. I am grateful that I have Your Spirit, and that I have purpose beyond myself. For in You I find all things, and in You I can rest in the plans and purposes of a big God. Amen.

Journal Page

God created me, and this makes me …

_____

_____

_____

_____

_____

_____

_____

_____

_____

_____

_____

_____

_____

_____

_____

_____

_____

_____

_____

_____

KEY POINTS FROM LESSON 5

- All of my days were written in God's book before my first breath.
- He has ordained my days—set forth by express design.
- I am a woman chosen by God and belonging to God.
- I am His work, His art, His poem, His masterpiece.
- I do not belong to myself, but have been created to live for God.
- The Lord desires to work in my life to seek and save the lost.
- All things in my life are working together for good.
- Nothing can separate me from God's love.
- I am alive in this moment of history, for such a time as this.
- My history is His Story in my life.
- I can trust in God's unfailing love.
- The Lord is always working on my behalf and working in me to will and do of His purpose.

Love Is My Foundation and My Confidence

LESSON 6

Do I trust at all in the flesh? Or have I learned to go beyond all confidence in myself and other people of God? Do I trust in books and prayers or other joys in my life? Or have I placed my confidence in God Himself, not in His blessings?

—OSWALD CHAMBERS

Blessed are those whose strength is in you.

—PSALM 84:5

hile looking up *foundation* in the dictionary, I found some descriptions that helped me understand w important a foundation is when building a relationship with a loving God. A foundation is a base the basis on which something stands.

Every woman has a foundation just as every building has a foundation. When the foundation is ak and unstable, the entire building is unstable. It is the same for us. When our foundation is weak, become unstable, anxious, and insecure. But when we are being built on a firm base, we will grow o firm, solid, secure women.

These days it is common to base our foundation on self. We are encouraged, "Learn to love your-lf. Trust yourself. Be strong and lean on yourself. If you believe in yourself, you can do anything." hile accepting yourself and embracing God's love for you is good, focusing on self is just another p that leads us to believe in ourselves for completeness.

The Bible tells us to *believe in God*. To believe that through His power all things are possible. he book of Proverbs tells us not to be wise in our own eyes and not to lean on our own under-anding. Yet even as Christian women we continue to rely solely on ourselves at times. The Bible

gives wisdom in an area we don't want to agree with, so we trust ourselves and pick and choo
whom and what we will believe. This is building our life not on a solid foundation but on ve
unstable ground.

As we learn to accept that we serve a loving God, we will learn that He can be absolutely trus
with our lives. Then we'll want to build our lives on His wisdom and His Word, rejoicing in
strength of His foundation.

 DAY ONE: A FIRM FOUNDATION

1. Read Matthew 7:24–27. Write the essence of these verses in your own words.

*"These words I speak to you are not incidental additions to your life, homeowner
improvements to your standard of living. They are foundational words, words
to build a life on. If you work these words into your life, you are like a smart
carpenter who built his house on solid rock. Rain poured down, the river flooded,
a tornado hit—but nothing moved that house. It was fixed to the rock.
"But if you just use my words in Bible studies and don't work them into your life,
you are like a stupid carpenter who built his house on the sandy beach. When a
storm rolled in and the waves came up, it collapsed like a house of cards."*

—MATTHEW 7:24–27 MSG

2. Write out Proverbs 14:1.

If you are to be a wise woman, what are some practical ways in which you can build your house on the foundational words of God?

What will happen if you build on the wrong foundation?

Have you purposed in your heart to believe the Bible as truth and to base your entire life on that truth as your solid foundation? What motivates you to do that, or what hinders you?

Read James 1:22–25. How is reading God's words like looking into a mirror?

What is the mirror meant to tell you about yourself?

How is ignoring God's words in practice like ignoring what you see in the mirror?

God says in His Word that He loves you and that your life has value. Do you tend to base your daily actions on those statements, or do you tend to ignore them in practice? Give an example of how you do that.

There is no better security than to have Christ as our foundation, our rock, our anchor. Then wh the storms of life come—and they will—we will remain standing. Life can be tough at times, a when our foundation is self, friends, family, or things, we are on shaky and unpredictable ground.

The Bible is a record of God working mightily in and through the lives of ordinary people. —Billy Graham

Anything other than our relationship with God can be taken fro us. That is one of the reasons that it is important to put all of our eg into one basket—Jesus Christ. Then we can know that no matter wh happens, we are solid and secure.

How many people do you know who are secure despite their c cumstances? How many women do you know who can laugh at t future, especially when none of us is certain about the circumstanc that will surround the future?

If we are going to be wise women, we must build our lives not on the sands of time, but on fai in Jesus Christ and His Word. Otherwise, we will be Nervous Nellies, anxiously living through ea day as if there were no God in heaven. Too many women live like this. But, ladies, good news: The is a God in heaven, and He cares for you!

Let the living God be your foundation. The Creator of all things is willing and able to give yo life the anchor and stability that it needs.

You may be asking yourself, *How do I have God as my foundation?* The answer is this: Daily lay yo life before God, allowing Him to then build on your surrendered heart.

The Lesson

Lord, for many months I prayed
To be filled with the Holy Spirit
That I might have more of Jesus.
But slowly you are teaching me
That to be filled with the Holy Spirit
Means that Jesus has all of me. [1]

—RUTH HARMS CALKIN

Lord,

There are so many things to build a life on in this world. I have often built on a fault line rather than a firm foundation. I want this to change. I want to be firmly built on the foundation of who You are and Christ's life in me. Amen.

 Day Two: Love Imparts Confidence

Read Proverbs 3:19–26.

What have God's wisdom and understanding accomplished?

According to this passage, what can the wisdom and understanding that come from God do in your life?

Confidence is a quality lacking in women today. Though confidence seminars abound now more an ever before, confidence is still some unattainable, unexplainable vapor in most women's lives. hat is confidence? The dictionary defines it this way:

—a feeling of trust

—faith

—a relationship of trustful intimacy

—fearlessness

—self-assuredness (self-confidence)

—a feeling of certainty

Building our life on an improper foundation equals building our life on uncertainty. If the Word God is not our foundation, we will be tossed by every circumstance. The opposite of confidence can described this way:

—low self-esteem

—fear

—insecurity

—lack of trust and faith

How can God's love impart confidence in us? Let's apply truth to the above definition of confiden[

A feeling of trust comes as we see God's faithfulness to us and to others as written in His Wo[
We begin to get the picture that He is a loving Father and that we can trust Him. We begin to see
pattern of how He works in and through people's lives, weaving His faithfulness in and out of e[
event with absolute purpose.

Faith comes by building ourselves up with the promises of His Word (faith comes by hearing
Word of God, Romans 10:17). We see that He has been faithful to His people from generation
generation. His love won't stop now! We can apply His words and His faithfulness to our lives o[
personal level.

> *Faith makes the Uplook Good*
> *The Outlook Bright*
> *The Inlook Favorable*
> *And the Future Glorious.[2]*
> —BARBARA JOHNSON

A relationship of trustful intimacy comes as we connect daily with God and make depending
Him a habit throughout the day. Personal relationship involves TIME. It involves talking to G[
thanking God, obeying His Word, and being up close and personal with Him!

> *All of us can know Him in this deeper sense. All of us have the unbelievable privilege*
> *of walking with the Lord of the Universe, of talking with Him daily, of asking Him*
> *to guide us, and expecting Him to enter into every facet of our lives. It's Jesus Christ*
> *Himself who invites you to look deeply into His loving eyes and take firm hold of His*
> *strong hands. He wants to keep you company as you walk through all of life.[3]*
> —GREG LAURIE

Fearlessness comes by building ourselves up with God's Word, which declares His love for us
God is for us, who can be against us? His Word talks of His loving protection again and again.

ed to realize that our lives are actually in His keeping. His nature is to lovingly care for us. When
e know these things, we grow in security and move a step away from fear.

> *We are afraid that the God who says He loves us will prove in the end to be more demanding*
> *than loving. I am convinced that the real reason we pray so little is fear: fear of facing God, fear*
> *also of facing our own and others' brokenness. I think our fearful hearts are saying: "Can I really*
> *trust God? Will He really show me His love when I don't keep anything hidden from Him?"* [4]
>
> —HENRI J. M. NOUWEN

As we begin to grasp His love for us, fear will become less of an issue in our lives. We will realize
at we can be real with our issues, our feelings, and our struggles. We will have confidence to trust in
oving, faithful God.

Self-assuredness comes as we learn who we are in Christ. We learn we have value and a place in this
orld, but apart from God we can accomplish nothing of eternal value. Our confidence soars as we
alize that in Him all things are possible, and we are in Him! It is the "I can do everything through
m who gives me strength" kind of confidence (Phil. 4:13). Paul says, "Let him who boasts boast in
e Lord" (1 Cor. 1:31). This is God-confidence—acceptance of self based on belief in God.

Finally, *a feeling of certainty* is the sense of knowing God's love and provision. It comes by meditating
 His Word and letting His Word sink into every pore and fiber of your being. It is an amazing peace
d confidence that comes from being certain you are loved and that your life is "Father-filtered."

All of the above add up to confidence in a sovereign, loving God who operates in grace and mercy!
e grow in confidence as we grow in an understanding of who He really is.

Write out the following verses. Say them to yourself as you write, so the truths sink in.
salm 54:4

salm 62:11–12

salm 63:3–5

Psalm 139:5

Think about Psalm 139:5. Really think about what it is saying for a moment. Imagine that t Lord goes before you and behind you and then lays His hand on you, as if to seal you. Isn't it wonderf to think of a God who encompasses us with Himself? Psalm 139:6 says that the very thought of this too much to understand, and the rest of the psalm goes on to explain how God is always with us.

Lord,
I thank You that You are my protector, my provider, and my peace. Amen.

 DAY THREE: CONFIDENCE IN GOD'S CARE

1. Read Psalm 139:6–12 once again. We're returning to this passage again and again, each tin letting it sink in deeper. Read slowly enough to let God speak to you afresh. What picture God and His care for you emerges when you read it this time?

• Does reading these verses build your confidence? How, or why not?

For many of us confidence is a struggle. Years of insecurity and fear keep us always at arm's leng from God. This distance hinders our ability to have confidence in Him and His love for us. He war to heal us from this pit of insecurity.

• Why do you suppose God would want to deliver you from feeling terrible about yourself and your lif

Does being insecure cause you to be a bit too self-focused at times? If so, how?

Does insecurity stop you from being completely God-centered? If so, give an example of how that works in your life.

Do your insecurities cause you to worry about pleasing people rather than living to please God? Give an example of how they do or don't.

Our insecurities can cause us to do crazy things. They can cause us to act in ways that are not compatible with God's Word and certainly not pleasing to Him. Sometimes insecurities can cause us lie, stretch the truth, be overly sensitive, gossip, separate friends, act arrogantly, have unbecoming attitudes, and so on. How do we get to the bottom of these insecurities, and let God and His Word ride more richly in our hearts and minds?

As we read in Romans 12:2, we must renew our thought patterns with the truth of God. This cannot be said enough. God's Word will do the work. The Bible says it is sharper than a two-edged word, able to cut away at our hearts!

Write out Hebrews 4:12 from your own Bible.

God means what he says. What he says goes. His powerful Word is sharp as a surgeon's scalpel,
cutting through everything, whether doubt or defense, laying us open to listen and obey. Nothing
and no one is impervious to God's Word. We can't get away from it—no matter what.

—HEBREWS 4:12 MSG

For every negative thing we hear or think, we need many more positives to counterbalance the ᴄ
single negative. That is why it is so important to fill up on God's promises. God's Word is the tru
We need to *know* His Word and be able to recall His words in an instant.

Years ago, while in the midst of an unexpected and unwanted divorce, I felt helpless, wound
and worthless. I suppose you could say I had no confidence at all. This feeling of failure caused
to plummet into despair to the point that I could not even grasp God. I could no longer relate to ᴌ
Word or His promises to me. During that time of darkness, several verses that I had memorized o
the years came back to my mind. I repeated those basic verses over and over to myself. Sometimᴇ
would say them in the hush of sobs, and other times I would say them out loud with enthusiasm. Aᴨ
a short while of just repeating the Word of God to myself, my spirits began to lift and I was able to tᴜ
my focus from self-pity and back to God and His love for me.

I then began reading Psalm 139 out loud each morning. Every day I was reminding myself w
my Maker was, how He was watching over me, and the fact that He had fashioned my days aᴨ
ordained them. All day I was filled with thoughts about the wonder of God and how His Word ᴡ
healing me and lifting me up to places where I never thought I would be able to go again becaᴜ
of the pain of divorce. God's Word truly can heal us from broken hearts. His Word is powerful
meeting our every need.

3. Write out Psalm 61:2.

As I look at Psalm 71:6 ("From birth I have relied on you"), I am prompted to ask God alᴡ
to be my confidence. From birth we all relied on God to keep our hearts beating and our lungs fil
with air. It was an unspoken reliance, but nevertheless it was reliance for life, pure and simple. Then

ew up, and many of us became so sophisticated that we forgot God and turned instead to people— arents, friends, other relatives. But because those people were imperfect humans just like us, they iled us, and we became afraid to trust anyone again. Think again—God can be trusted! He has ept us for many years. It was He who brought us forth out of our mother's womb, and He can be our onfidence. Remember: Confidence in God = security.

> *Separated from God and His Word, people have only their abilities and*
> *the opinions of others on which to base their worth, and the circumstances*
> *around them ultimately control the way they feel about themselves.[5]*
> —ROBERT MCGEE

Read Romans 1:20–25. What do the following statements have to say about our search for meaning and confidence?
lthough they claimed to be wise, they became fools

hey exchanged the truth of God for a lie

hey worshipped things and people rather than the Creator

Did you ever stop to think how it is so incredible that we look to others to discover our worth hen their perspective is as limited and darkened as our own? We need instead to rely on God's steady nd uplifting Word to discover who we are and what we are worth. Ask God to help you look only to Iim for approval, and ask Him to tear down the lies you have believed about yourself. *Exchange those es for His truth!*

Understanding we have a loving God compels us to action, because when we know we are loved, e want to respond to that love by living a life pleasing to Him. And as we grow in our understanding f God's nature and His love for His people, we will grow in confidence and trust.

Lord,
May You always be my confidence. May I always look only to You for approval.
May I always put You first in my life. Amen.

 DAY FOUR: TRUTH AND SECURITY = HOPE

1. Read the following verses and then write down the adjectives they use to describe God. T
more you come to know of His nature, the more secure you will be.
Psalm 111:4

Exodus 34:6–7

We need to know the truth in more than just an intellectual way. We need to allow God's truth
penetrate the most basic parts of our lives, such as our motives, goals, sense of self-worth, and con
dence. In many cases, God's love has only touched the surface and has not yet penetrated our deep
thoughts and beliefs about ourselves. Often these misbeliefs reflect misperceptions such as these:
- God doesn't really care about me.
- I am an unlovable, worthless person. Nobody will ever love me.
- I'll never be able to change.
- I've been a failure all my life. I guess I'll always be a failure.
- If people really knew me, they wouldn't like me.

> *When the light of love and honesty shines on thoughts of hopelessness, it is often very*
> *painful. We begin to admit that we really do feel negatively about ourselves, and have*
> *for a long time. But, God's love, expressed through His people, and woven into our*
> *lives by His Spirit and His Word can, over a period of time, bring healing even to*
> *our deepest wounds and instill within us an appropriate sense of self-worth.*[6]
>
> —ROBERT MCGEE

Read 2 Corinthians 5:14–15. According to these verses, whom are you supposed to live for? Why?

Write out Proverbs 3:26.

Before God can build our lives securely, He must lay a foundation. We need a solid, secure, strong se. In order to have the materials for this foundation, we must be in God's Word. To understand love our foundation, we must read of His love for us and meditate on the truth.

> *When it comes to the major-league difficulties like death, disease, sin, and*
> *disaster—you know that God cares. But what about the smaller things? What*
> *about grouchy bosses or flat tires or lost dogs? What about broken dishes, late*
> *flights, toothaches, or a crashed hard drive? Do these matter to God?*
> *I mean, He's got a universe to run. He's got the planets to keep balanced*
> *and presidents and kings to watch over. He's got wars to worry about and*
> *famines to fix. Who am I to tell Him about my ingrown toenail?*
> *I'm glad you asked. Let me tell you who you are.*
> *In fact, let me proclaim who you are.*
> *You are an heir of God and a co-heir with Christ.*
> *You are eternal, like an angel.*
> *You have a crown that will last forever.*
> *You are a holy priest, a treasured possession.*
> *But more than any of the above—more significant than any title or*
> *position—is the simple fact that you are God's child.[7]*
>
> —MAX LUCADO

God's child? Now that's an inheritance! If we truly believe what is true about us, and about our Go
our foundation will be as firm as the strongest concrete. In fact, that is exactly what it will be like.

4. Write out Joshua 1:8.

5. Write out Psalm 119:9.

6. Read Psalm 136 out loud. What is the repeated theme of this psalm?

In Proverbs 23:7 (KJV) we read, "For as [she] thinketh in [her] heart, so is [she]." From this prove
we can conclude that we must get to the very heart of the matter—our thoughts and attitudes.
Robert McGee states in his book *Search for Significance*, we have a choice. We can either continue
evaluate our worth based on the world's standards: **confidence/self-worth = performance and ot
ers' opinions.** Or we can judge our worth by God's standards: **confidence/self-worth = God's tru
about me.** If we want to live as God intended, we must embrace His truth as our measuring tool.

7. Write out Hebrews 10:35.

Don't throw away the truth of God's Word, which can give you confidence in yourself! This week ›mind yourself daily: His love endures forever.

In embracing the Word of God and meditating on the truth, we tear down the negative images nd messages on which we have built our lives in the past. God is all-powerful and can use even the ›metimes-ugly events of our pasts to help mold us into the strong, God-confident women that He has ›esigned us to be. I emphasize being God-confident because having absolute confidence in God needs › be the firm foundation on which all else can then be securely built.

Think of a house. We are building our house on the Rock, Jesus Christ. Confidence in God is our ›ew foundation. This leads to confidence in ourselves, the women He is making us to be, because we ›e in Him. And we have respect for ourselves because we realize our value and worth in His plan. ›hese two together add up to the freedom to reach out to others in true humility and love. We become ›omen who are no longer bound but free to be ourselves. When this freedom is a result of growing in ›iblical truths, then we are set free indeed.

Lord,
When I think of putting my confidence in You, I have peace. Teach me what it means to allow You control over my construction site—my life. Show me how to ensure a solid foundation. Amen.

     DAY FIVE: THE ARMOR OF LOVE

. **Write out Ephesians 6:10.**

What do you think it means to "be strong in the Lord"?

- Is God's mighty power your foundation? Why, or why not?

- Are you strong? What makes you say that?

- What is the source of your strength?

2. Write out Ephesians 6:11.

- What is "the full armor of God"?

3. Read Ephesians 6:12–17. What are your thoughts on the following statements?
We struggle

We need armor

The days are evil

e need His Word to stand

ke your stand against the devil's schemes

To stand firm, Jesus Christ must be our foundation! Some of us have no foundation at all. We ep trying to build on a mound of debris. We may once have had a solid foundation, but some- here along the way it was torn up and discarded. Perhaps you need a new foundation poured so at your life might be built on the security of Christ Jesus.

> *We can forget about God. Oh, we don't stop loving God. We don't stop believing in God. But quite honestly, we forget about Him. Remember that no matter how noble or good a certain thing is in and of itself, anything that comes between us and Jesus can become sin. We must not become so preoccupied with religious activity that we forget about Jesus. We should hate to take a single step without Him. Like Jesus, we too must be about our Father's business—and we won't manage that unless we walk with Him every moment of our lives.* [8]
> —GREG LAURIE

We learn to stand firm in the truth by looking at everything in light of God's Word. The Bible comes our standard. If thoughts come to our minds that are contrary to the truth in God's ord, we must dismiss them. We must say, "No! I believe what God says about me, my life, and y future."

It is time that we live in the truth on a daily basis. Only then will we be set free!

Think about the children's story "The Three Little Pigs." What do you remember about it?

Well, obviously there was a big bad wolf, and maybe you have had some big bad wolves in your life o. They may not be people; the wolves might be circumstances that have become so overwhelming to u that you're sure your little house will collapse at any moment. This is where the rubber meets the ad. Will the hardships of life do you in? Satan certainly is set on huffing and puffing and blowing ur house down! But Jesus Christ has overcome the world and Satan's power. Is your foundation Jesus hrist today?

4. Write out Psalm 36:7, 10.

Isn't it amazing how much God loves you? You are precious to Him—that's what His Word sa
He thinks about you so much that you cannot even begin to count the endless thoughts He has abc
you. And you wake up each day because you are in His hands. This is a loving Father, one in whom y
can totally trust. His love for you must be the foundation of your life. Everything else will spring fo
from this foundation of love and acceptance.

> *All that we build is going to be inspected by God. When God inspects us with His searching*
> *and refining fire, will He detect that we have built enterprises of our own on the foundation of*
> *Jesus? We are living in a time of tremendous enterprises, a time when we are trying to work for*
> *God, and that is where the trap is. Profoundly speaking, we can never work for God. Jesus, as a*
> *Master Builder, takes us over so that He may direct and control us completely for His enterprises*
> *and His building plans; and no one has any right to demand where he will be put to work.[9]*
>
> —OSWALD CHAMBERS

Dear Lord,
Many things around me scream for my attention. Things that seem right in
themselves. But some of these things don't lead me closer to You. In fact, some
just lead me to trusting myself. Father, I don't want to base my life on me. I
want to base my life on You.

Thank You for working in me, causing me to desire You and Your strong,
firm base as the security for my life. I love You! Make me now a woman of
confidence, security, and strength. Do this work in me by the power of Your
Holy Spirit and by the building of a firm foundation. Amen.

Journal Page

Oh, that we would be women who turn our eyes from the worthless, vain, worldly foundations that have made us insecure, weak, and fearful. What are your worthless things?

_____

_____

_____

_____

_____

_____

_____

_____

_____

_____

_____

_____

_____

_____

_____

_____

_____

_____

_____

_____

_____

Key Points from Lesson 6

- In order to be stable, my life must be built on a firm foundation.
- Jesus Christ, according to Scripture, is that firm foundation.
- When my life is not on the foundation of Christ, anything can topple me.
- It's wise to build on Christ, and stupid to build on other things.
- Confidence is a trust, faith, intimacy, fearlessness, and certainty in God.
- God covers me much like the shelter of the borders of a box around me.
- God's Word is powerful and cuts into the depths of my brokenness.
- Jesus is my healer.
- I am to live for an audience of one—pleasing God.
- I am not to worship things—but instead worship the Creator.
- There is a battle and God has equipped me with all I need.
- I must put on the armor of love each day.
- The Lord is my confidence.
- His love endures forever.

Love Corrects Me

LESSON 7

The Holy Spirit will show you what to do, and it will involve anything that will uproot what is preventing you from getting through to Jesus.

—OSWALD CHAMBERS

The Lord disciplines those he loves.

—HEBREWS 12:6

a parent I am constantly challenged by the fact that I am shaping lives on a daily basis. In love it's portant for me to help my children, correcting them when they make mistakes and giving them nfidence to soar. In the same way the Lord God, our heavenly Father, shapes our lives each day. In the ocess of shaping, He too corrects us when we are in error and gives us confidence to soar to higher places Him. Every correction we receive from the Lord is part of His shaping our lives into His design.

My children love me, but they certainly don't like to be corrected. Nobody is thrilled with a triction or a time-out. But sometimes that's exactly what we need. Sometimes our circumstances trict us, nudging us to look into an area of our lives where God is dealing with us. Sometimes cumstances force us into a time-out, and though we don't want to sit in a chair in the corner of the om, staring at every spot on the wall, sitting there may be exactly the way God gets our attention. ace He has our attention, He can lovingly correct us.

We must keep in mind that even though God corrects us, His love never changes toward us. There re times when my children were younger that they would storm out of the room after I had corrected m, saying, "You just don't love me, Mom!" Nothing could have been further from the truth. My e for them didn't change; it was just taking a shape that they didn't like at that moment.

God's love for us never changes. But His love isn't always warm and fuzzy. Part of His love involves correction and discipline. In fact, Scripture says this is one of the ways we know we are His daughters and that He loves us.

 DAY ONE: CORRECTION PRODUCES CHANGE

1. The Bible often uses the word *discipline*. Look up the definition of *discipline* in your dictionary. Write it here.

• Look up the definitions of *correct* and *correction* in your dictionary. Write them here.

2. Write out Proverbs 3:11–12.

3. Read Hebrews 12:1–13. Summarize what you think these verses are saying to you.

Our sufferings may be rough and hard to bear, but they teach us lessons, which in turn equip and enable us to help others. Our attitude toward suffering should not be, "Grit your teeth and bear it," hoping it will pass as quickly as possible. Rather, our goal should be to learn all we can from what we are called upon to endure.[1]

—BILLY GRAHAM

Write out Hebrews 12:1.

This verse compares life to a race. Read the verse again—out loud. Then journal what God is speaking to you through the following words:

brow off everything that hinders

be sin that so easily entangles

et us run with perseverance

be race marked out for us

Runners wear non-binding clothing when they race. They wear nothing that will hinder their erformance during the run and nothing that will stop them from reaching their goal. They also run ith patience, even though many parts of the course are less than thrilling. Despite what they feel, they ay focused on their goal of making it across the finish line.

Do you think you could keep running a race if you had a pebble in your running shoe? Why, or why not?

It would be wise to stop, take the rock out, lace the shoe up again, and get back on track. How do we do that in the race of the Christian life?

Lord,

Sometimes it seems like I am going strong and then something stops me in my tracks. Help me realize that I can start over as many times as necessary on my journey with You. I need You and all that You have promised to be in and through me. Amen.

 **Day Two: Undivided Focus**

1. Read Hebrews 12:2. Read it again—out loud. Then journal what God is speaking to y **through the following words.**

Let us fix our eyes on Jesus

Turn your eyes upon Jesus.

Look full in His wonderful face

And the things of earth will grow strangely dim

In the light of His glory and grace.

—Helen H. Lemmel

The author and perfecter of our faith

Who for the joy set before him endured the cross

• Are your eyes fixed on Jesus today? Why, or why not?

What does the runner do to get to the finish line?
• She fixes her mind on the finish line.
• She concentrates on the path before her.
• She focuses on running the race.

Our life is like a race and Jesus is the finish line; therefore, we are to fix our eyes on Jesus. O mind is to be set on God and His purposes.

Read Psalm 119:34–37. Write out key thoughts.

Are you focusing on unimportant or worthless things? Explain.

Jesus is the author and perfecter of our faith. I find this encouraging, because I don't have to per-t faith within myself. The Word says Jesus is the beginning and the end.

Write out Philippians 1:6.

> You are His gem—tested, shining and sparkling. You have survived the winds of adversity.... You are a winner! You are an overcomer! You have credentials!
> —Source Unknown

Another reason for confidence! The God who loves us, who never changes, will complete His work us. (There is a reason we keep repeating this verse.)

For the joy set before Him, He endured. That should be our attitude today.

Father,
How I praise You that I can put all of my trust in You. You correct me, but it is always for my good. Work in me. Amen.

Day Three: All Things

Write out Romans 8:28.

• Does it give you joy to know that God is working *all* things together for good in your life? Expla

2. Now write out Romans 8:29.

• According to this verse, what good is being produced in you through the circumstances of life?

• What do you think it means "to be conformed to the image of his Son"?

> *God loves you just the way you are, but He refuses to leave you there. He wants you to be just like Jesus.*
> *Isn't that good news? You aren't stuck with today's personality. You aren't condemned to grumpy-dom.*
> *You are changeable. You are tweakable. Even if you've worried each day of your life, you needn't worry*
> *the rest of your life. So what if you were born with a sour outlook, you don't have to die with one.*
> *God will change you. And He will change you to be just like Jesus. Can you think of a better offer?* [2]
>
> —MAX LUCADO

• What are some areas in which you know God wants to work?

• Can you go to God with these areas today? If not, why not?

If we were just like Jesus, we would be women of love. We would see the best, believe the best, and pe in the best. We would also be women of faith. We would know that God is faithful to every one 'His promises. Need some changing? I do.

Read Hebrews 12:3–5. Read this passage again—out loud. Then journal what God is speaking to you through the following words:

onsider him … so that you will not grow weary and lose heart

your struggle … you have not yet resisted to the point of shedding blood

ou have forgotten the word of encouragement that addresses you as [daughters]

y [daughter], do not make light of the Lord's discipline

o not lose heart when he rebukes you

Write out Hebrews 12:6.

Read this verse again—out loud. Then journal what God is speaking to you through the following words:
he Lord disciplines [corrects] those he loves

e punishes everyone he accepts as a [daughter]

Praise Upon Praise

O Father
Through the years
You have permitted
Hurt upon hurt
In my God-planned life.
This early morning
Even before I greet the dawn
I offer You
Praise upon praise
For You are transforming every hurt
Into a holy hallmark—
A genuine guarantee
Of my permanent identification
With You.[3]

—RUTH HARMS CALKIN

Father,
I know You are at work in me, and that it is Your desire to make me like Jesus.
Be my everything. Amen.

 DAY FOUR: ENDURING HARDSHIP

1. Read Hebrews 12:7–8. Read these verses again—out loud. Then journal what God is speaki
to you through the following words:

Endure hardship as discipline [correction]

d is treating you as [daughters]

r what [daughter] is not disciplined by [her] father?

ou are not disciplined, then you are illegitimate children

The father-daughter connection may be a hard one for some of you to swallow. Many women not have good relationships with their fathers. Some women were even abandoned or abused as ildren. If you were hurt in some way by your natural father, that pain goes very deep and may span any years. That hurt makes it difficult for you to understand this idea of a father who loves.

Maybe you were disciplined, but not out of love. I have talked to women who had the daylights aten out of them as children. That certainly is not the kind of love-discipline relationship the ole is referring to here. It might be helpful right now to put everything down and pray that God ll make real to you what He is to you as a Father—and how much He loves you.

Read Hebrews 12:9–10. Read these verses again—out loud. Then journal what God is speak-ng to you through the following words:
have all had human fathers who disciplined us

w much more should we submit to the Father of our spirits and live!

r fathers disciplined us … as they thought best

d disciplines us for our good, that we may share in his holiness

It's not enough for Him to own you; He wants to change you. Where you and I might be satisfied with a recliner and refrigerator, He refuses to settle for any dwelling short of a palace. After all, this is His house. No expense is spared. No corners are cut. "Oh the utter extravagance of his work in us who trust him" (Ephesians 1:19 MSG).

This might explain some of the discomfort in your life. Remodeling of the heart is not always pleasant. We don't object when the Carpenter adds a few shelves, but He's been known to gut the entire west wing. He has such high aspirations for you. God envisions a complete restoration. He won't stop until He is finished. And He won't be finished until we have been shaped "along the … lines … of his Son" (Romans 8:29 MSG).[4]

—MAX LUCADO

3. Write out Hebrews 12:11.

• Read this verse again—out loud. Then journal what God is speaking to you through the follow.
words.

No discipline seems pleasant at the time

But painful

Later on … it produces a harvest of righteousness and peace

For those who have been trained by it

Father,

So often I feel out of control. Help me to believe that even when I can't see the end, You have the end in sight and You are shaping me for Your good and glory. Amen.

 DAY FIVE: LEVEL PATHS

Write out Hebrews 12:12–13.

Read these verses again—out loud. Then journal what God is speaking to you through the following words:

rengthen your feeble arms and weak knees

'ake level paths for your feet

that the lame may not be disabled, but rather healed

Read Psalm 139:2–4 again. This psalm also expresses how God is ever present with us, and knows our words and deeds.

Read Revelation 3:15–19. This is a pretty intense statement of the fact that God knows all, and He may not be pleased with what He knows. Self-sufficient people don't realize their need.

- According to Revelation 3:15–19, what will God do to the church of Laodicea as a result of H disappointment with her deeds?

- Write out Revelation 3:19.

- According to Revelation 3:19, what goes hand in hand with God's love?

- What does God tell us to do because of this?

3. Read Revelation 3:20. God stands at the door of your heart today. Do you need to repent something? (Repenting is turning away from something, going in another direction.) What is i

We often think of repenting in terms of "BIG" sins. But God tells us we need to notice any of o attitudes and actions that aren't pleasing to God. They may not be big things to others, but if He convicting your heart, then you need to repent and turn away from that attitude or action.

4. Read Jeremiah 18:1–6.

We are all being shaped by the discipline of our heavenly Father. He shapes and molds us as a potter do clay on a potter's wheel. Being shaped is sometimes uncomfortable, but the end result is a masterpiece.

God shapes our lives as it seems best to Him. Often His ways make no sense to us, but we must remember that He is God, and we are not. Part of the problem with New Age philosophy is that people us all their energy on shaping themselves into something important and worthwhile. Psalm 127:1 's that unless the Lord shapes us, it is in vain. You and I don't know what shape our lives are meant take, but the God who created us knows full well. I would much rather trust my life to the One who he Author of it, the Creator of it, than to anyone or anything else.

If the LORD delights in a [woman's] way,
he makes [her] steps firm;
though [she] stumble, [she] will not fall,
for the LORD upholds [her] with his hand.

—PSALM 37:23–24

Dear Lord,
There are so many things in me that need Your touch. Help me to trust You when Your touch has to be less than gentle. I realize that You are working in me and using my circumstances to make me more like You—and I thank You for that. Just help me to keep my focus on You and Your purposes. Lord, I do want to be more like You. In fact, I want to be just like You. I submit to the work of Your Spirit and ask You to do Your grand and glorious work in my life. Amen.

Journal Page

- This week I have been thinking about discipline …

- God corrects those He loves.
- To experience change means to experience correction.
- I must run the race of life focused on Christ.
- An undivided heart and focus is important.
- I must train myself to "look up."
- Everything is part of the training and shaping of me into His vessel.
- He punishes me as necessary, and thereby shows Himself to be my loving heavenly Father.
- All discipline is for my good.
- Discipline not fun in the moment—but the fruit is more of Jesus and less of me.

Love Changes Me

How can we maintain the simplicity of Jesus so that we may understand Him?
By receiving His Spirit, recognizing and relying on Him, and obeying Him as
He brings us the truth of His word, life will become amazingly simple.

—OSWALD CHAMBERS

Being confident of this, that he who began a good work in you will carry it on to completion.

—PHILIPPIANS 1:6

ost of us want to change. Proof of this is the varied menu of growth and self-improvement courses
ered in churches, colleges, and community groups. Part of the reason we desire change is because,
ether we realize it or not, we desire growth. When we are growing, our lives are moving forward and
experience direction and fulfillment.

One of the synonyms of *change* is *transform*. In our study, we have been paying close attention to
e word *transformation*. As Romans 12:2 says, we are not to be conformed to this world but *trans-
med* by the renewing of our minds. We can conclude then that we will be changed as we grow in
r relationship with God. Do you want or need change today?

God loves to decorate. God has to decorate. Let him live long enough in a heart, and
that heart will begin to change. Portraits of hurt will be replaced by landscapes of
grace. Walls of anger will be demolished and shaky foundations restored. God can no
more leave a life unchanged than a mother can leave her child's tear untouched.[1]

—MAX LUCADO

 DAY ONE: JESUS MAKES THE DIFFERENCE

1. Look up *change* in the dictionary. Write the definition here.

There are two definitions of change that I find meaningful: to make different; to exchange.

I am so grateful that by the power of the Holy Spirit I can be different. The Lord needs to upr
certain things within me if my life is going to grow and bear fruit. I also love the idea of *exchar*
because God exchanged Jesus' life that I might have abundant life. He will also exchange His nat
for my selfish nature when I ask Him to do so. My part is coming to Him with myself.

> *How easy it is to fall into the trap of making a bold profession of a vital spiritual*
> *life when our number-one priority is seeking to please the flesh! Certainly the power*
> *that our fallen nature can hold over us is one of the biggest problems we face in life.*
> *How can we be free from the seemingly unconquerable bondage to the flesh?*
> *The simple yet profound answer is this: Don't fight the flesh, strengthen*
> *the Spirit! Don't fight against the darkness; turn on the light.[2]*
>
> —CHUCK SMITH

2. Write out Hebrews 4:16.

• Lesson 6 dealt with confidence. In Hebrews 4:16 you are instructed to approach God with co
dence. What do you think that means?

As we grow in our understanding of God's love, we will feel more comfortable going to Him with all our weaknesses and insecurities. When we go to Him, we find grace to help us in our everyday needs. The grace of God will do for us what we could never do for ourselves. That is the exchanged life!

Every day we have choices to make. Sometimes we make wise choices, and sometimes we make questionable choices. In either case, we all have things in our lives that cause us great anxiety. Some of these can be changed. We all obsess at times over things that are not changeable, and we need to learn accept those things that we cannot change and focus on the ones that we can.

In order to release some of these target areas to God, it will be helpful for you to take a personal inventory.

- Make a list of all the things you don't like about yourself or your life. Be specific.
- Now go through that list and put a check by all the things that cannot be changed. You need to commit those things to God. They cannot be changed; you must learn to trust God with them and accept them.
- Make a second list that includes everything from the first list that does not have a check. These are the things that can be changed. This is your new target list. This list should become a focus in your prayers.

Now spend some time praying about the inventory you just finished. First, give God all the things that cannot be changed. You must accept these things because they cannot change. No amount of self-pity will change them, but your acceptance of them will give you a new attitude about them. Give them and your attitude to God, and ask Him to give you the grace to accept the things you cannot change.

Next, take the new list and look it over closely. You may have several things on your list that can actually change—such as disorganization, procrastination, hairstyle, weight, etc. (For most women much of this list revolves around appearances or performance. Sadly, we spend so much energy looking at the outside, don't we? Have you included on your list the inside things that are probably God's priorities for transforming you?) With this new list in hand, the first thing you need to do is admit the fact that though you have tried changing some of these areas in the past, you have been unsuccessful. This time you need to start by asking God for His power to work in you in all these areas. You need to concentrate on drawing close to Him, turning on the light in areas that have been dark! Your spirit needs to be fed, filled, and strengthened.

Some things may have been dragging you down for years, and the distraction of never dealing with the has caused more anxiety than they're worth. It seems common for us to think that we have to live with all our bad habits and basic "yuck." Evidently, some of us have bought into the idea that if God wants it change He will just change it. But we have choices regarding the changeable things that keep us down. Every d God allows us to make choices. The most important choice of each day is walking in His Spirit.

When we walk in the Spirit, living in constant awareness of the presence of God, we no longer need others to nag and preach at us about living up to Christian standards. Our lives will be revolutionized as we keep the nearness and love of God in the front of our minds.[3]

—CHUCK SMITH

Our personal areas of struggle can continue to keep us self-focused, or we can ask God for F wisdom and strength in dealing with those particular problems. Choose today to make the wise choice—surrendering to God for His help and strength.

Proverbs 3:6 says, "In all your ways acknowledge him, and *he will make your paths straight.*" Cou this mean that in Him you can find the direction you need to help you with the weaknesses a change your life? You bet!

God grant me the serenity To accept the things I cannot change The courage to change the things I can And the wisdom to know the difference.[4]

—REINHOLD NIEBUHR

3. Write out John 16:33.

• What does John 16:33 say you will have in this life? What does this mean?

What attitude does this verse say you should have toward a less-than-perfect life?

Why are you to have cheer?

Look at this definition of *cheer* from *Webster's:* good spirits; "something providing happiness or joy; couragement; to fill with happiness." With this definition in mind, think of what it might mean to of good cheer. You can be filled with happiness and joy and be encouraged in your spirit, because d has overcome the world and all of those unchangeable challenges that we face.

The Greek word in this passage is *tharseo,* which means to have courage, strength. Courage mes from knowing Jesus and trusting that He is working in and through all things that touch my lividual life.

Sometimes I throw my own pity party. Instead of balloons and cupcakes, I have Kleenex and rs—all because I cannot get a handle on a particular situation, and I just want it fixed today. The y party approach is in contrast to the cheer approach I see here in God's Word. The pity party isn't a ebration of courage but rather a statement of discouragement. I need to climb out of the pit of pity as ickly as I can. It is a trap that leads to the exact opposite of cheer. Part of God's changing me is a radi- change in perspective as a result of a different life focus and the empowering of God's Holy Spirit.

Satan's first attack on the human race was his sly effort to destroy Eve's confidence in God's kindness. om that day, people have had false conceptions of God. Nothing twists and deforms the soul more than)w or unworthy concept of God. The god of the Pharisees was not a god easy to live with.

From a failure to properly understand God comes a world of unhappiness among Christians even lay. The Christian life is thought to be a glum, unrelieved cross-carrying under the eye of a stern her who expects much and excuses nothing.

The truth is that God is the most winsome of all beings and His service one of unspeakable pleasure. He loves us for ourselves and values our love more than galaxies of new created worlds.[5]
—A. W. TOZER

We don't need to be throwing pity parties. Ladies, God loves us, and He is in control!

Lord,
Every time I begin to go into self-pity, remind me that the pity party is catered by Satan and his lying demons. This reminder will encourage me to stop the spiral before it can get started. My desire is to have cheer in You! Amen.

 DAY TWO: STEP BY STEP

1. Read Philippians 4:4–13.
• These verses give some instructions for accepting life's circumstances. Write out the instructi~~ons~~
  you see.
Example: Rejoice.

• Now write the promises that go with following these instructions.
Example: I will have peace.

2. Write out Philippians 4:19.

• How will the way you approach life be different if this is true?

3. Read John 16:33 again. Jesus was warning His disciples that life would be difficult. Why w~~as~~ He doing this?

In this world you will have tribulation. This is reality. Troubles. Affliction. Distress.

Father,
Because I can't change the fact that hardships are a fact of life, help me to remember that You are in control and that in You I can overcome. Amen.

 DAY THREE: STRENGTHENED AND SETTLED

Write out 1 Peter 5:10.

Instead of promising you that He will change all the circumstances of your life, what does God promise you in 1 Peter 5:10?

Hard times can be tools to shape us into greater strength, to change us. Once we have come to cept that some situations, people, or things cannot be changed, we learn to be content. It's like haling—letting out all that steam that kept us bound in frustration before.

Now we will look at trusting God in the things that can be changed.

Read John 14. Write out verse 16. Remember that the Holy Spirit is your source for change.

As we have previously studied, the Holy Spirit is called our Helper. The same Holy Spirit that Jesus talks about here in the book of John indwells each believer. It's awesome to think that I have with me the Holy Spirit of God.

Often we forget that God's Spirit has been given to us. Scripture tells us we weren't left as orphan but we have received the Spirit of God. Recently, I have made it a practice to remind myself every d that the Holy Spirit indwells me. It's an exciting adventure to watch the Holy Spirit work through r in the daily things of life.

> *In great simplicity and restfulness believe in Him as having given His own Spirit within you. Accept this as the secret of the life of Christ in you: the Holy Spirit is dwelling in the hidden recesses of your spirit. Meditate on it, believe Jesus and His word concerning it, until your soul bows with holy fear and awe before God under the glory of the truth: the Holy Spirit of God is, indeed, dwelling in me. Yield yourself to His leading. We have seen that leading is not just in the mind or thoughts, but in the life and disposition. Yield yourself to God, to be guided by the Holy Spirit in all your conduct.[6]*
>
> —ANDREW MURRAY

In this New Age era, it's not uncommon to hear that we need to ask "a spirit to guide us" or that should "pray to the light." What spirit, and what light? The light of yourself? The spirit of the univers Sadly, in the rush to find our purpose and dip into some spirituality, many of us are paying big buc to get in touch with ourselves and/or some spiritual guide.

How wonderful that as Christians we need to search no more! Jesus Christ is the Light, and F gave us His Spirit to be our Guide. Best of all, we don't have to pay big bucks for what God has free given. In John 14:6 Jesus says, "I am the way and the truth and the life."

I am excited to live in tune with the Holy Spirit of God, relying on the Holy Spirit's power to gi me the strength I need in all areas of life. Sadly, like everyone else, I forget to rely on the Holy Spi as much as I should. I let areas go unchecked and unchanged, because they just seem so overwhelmi and hard for me to change and because I forget that through Christ all things are possible. I keep tr ing on my own and end up running out of steam. *Hello? Is anyone there? Where am I to go for help?*

Today I challenge you to continually rely on the Holy Spirit of God for every area of change th showed up on your inventory list earlier in this lesson. As I challenge you, I also challenge myself. F it is time that we take hold of what Christ has promised us and live in the fullness of His strength a the fullness of His Spirit's power.

Write out John 16:13–14.

Change is the by-product of growth.

G	God
R	Restoring
O	Our
W	Whole life
T	Through
H	His Son, Jesus

Growth does not happen overnight; it happens in small increments over a period of time. I like to nk of it as baby steps. But growth is not possible unless the conditions are right. Just as a garden is wn with proper nurturing and care, so the growth in our lives is produced with the proper attach-nt to the Vine. We don't make the fruit appear, for we cannot produce it in and of ourselves. Our t is staying attached to the Source of life and power who can produce beautiful and lasting fruit.

> *These days you can send messages across the world at the speed of light. You can cross*
> *the Atlantic in under three hours. You can microwave a whole meal in minutes. You*
> *can even get your dry cleaning back the same day! We move in a fast-paced society*
> *where everything is now. We don't want to wait. We ask for it and it's there.*
> *Sometimes we try to carry over that attitude to our relationship with God. We wonder, What*
> *are the shortcuts? What are the easy angles? What's the inside track? I'm sorry, but there aren't*
> *any shortcuts, there are no angles. The only way to spiritual growth is to abide. Sink your roots*
> *deeply into Jesus Christ and continually walk with Him, and in time you will see fruit.[7]*
>
> —GREG LAURIE

Lord,

There are so many areas that can be changed in my life. I surrender myself to

You for You to have Your way with me. Change me, Lord, and mold me. Help me understand that growth happens in baby steps, one step and one day at a time. Amen.

 DAY FOUR: CONNECTION = POWER

1. Read John 15. Write out verse 5.

• What does John 15 say happens in your life when you abide or remain in Christ?

• What happens when you are apart from Him?

Abiding in Christ is having a relationship with Him. Remember the three *Rs* from the beginn of the study?

REMAIN

RENEW

REST

The very first *R* is Remain, and it is the most important one. To remain in Christ is to abide Him, live in Him, be connected to Him. I like to think of myself as daily connecting to the Po▼ Source of life. When I think of it that way, I get a surge of excitement and anticipation each morni It is living a God-dependent life.

When I am tempted with the thoughts, *you can't do that, you don't have enough skill, it is too hard you … etc.,* I am able to say, "All things are possible for those who abide in Christ." I am so empowe the strength of God as I make that statement and add to it, "apart from Him I am nothing." These words have become my motto. They empower me because they remind me to stay close, connected, and attached to Him. They remind me daily to REMAIN, and then I am RENEWED, and as a result I can REST. My life is then in the growth phase, on the road to restoration, and things do begin to change!

And though it's true that we can "do" many things, we must realize that we can do nothing of eternal value that will honor Christ and bring life-changing restorative power apart from Christ and His Spirit at work within us. Yes, we have gifts, talents, and abilities, but think of the power in which those natural abilities can be used when submitted to Christ. It's like turning on the voltage. When we abide in Christ, we are using our gifts and abilities for His purposes, empowered by the Source much bigger, wiser, and mightier than ourselves.

Write out Galatians 5:22–23.

This fruit is the very nature of the Holy Spirit. It's important that we learn it, and not just in our heads. This fruit can be a key in receiving the power to walk in the Spirit.

Let's suppose that one of the areas of change you are praying about is your harshness. The Bible tells us here that the fruit of the Spirit is gentleness and kindness. So you can boldly and confidently ask the Holy Spirit of God to work within you, filling you with the strength and power of God. Our prayer should be for the exchange to happen. That is, that He would exchange the harshness for gentleness and kindness by His Spirit working within you, and by His Spirit convicting you and leading you on the pathway to change.

Read Psalm 18. Circle or underline all the times that David refers to strength. (This psalm was written while David was in battle. Likewise, when you are trying to conquer old, bad, and ingrained habits you are in battle! Just as the Lord was David's source of strength, so He can be yours today.)

Write out Psalm 68:19.

• According to this verse, who daily bears your burdens? What does this mean?

Lord,
I can do nothing unless I remain in You. Please help me to make time today to be aware of Your presence. Teach me to pray and to listen. Deepen my connection with You. Amen.

 DAY FIVE: SEEKING HIS STRENGTH

1. Write out the following verses:

Psalm 29:11

Psalm 84:5

Psalm 105:4

You cannot change everything at once. We tend to want to fix things immediately. Even the thin that can be changed need to be taken one by one to the Lord for His direction and strength. He c give us plans for change because He knows the entire situation better than anyone else. If deep-root problems are lurking and preventing change, guess who knows? He gives us a plan by directing us His Word and by bringing light to areas that were formerly dark or confused.

In this lesson, you compiled a list of changeable things. I suggest you take from that list the thi that drags you down the most and start there. Make that one area your point of prayer today. *Cautic* Don't try to change yourself in your own power. Just trust that God, by His grace, will give you wh you need to change one area at a time. He will meet you in the most exciting and practical ways.

Remember: "'Not by might nor by power, but by my Spirit,' says the LORD almighty" (Zech. 4:6). must trust in the God who never changes!

Write out Malachi 3:6. Underline the key words.

Write out Hebrews 13:8. Underline the key words.

May the God of all peace give you His strength as you trust Him for change in your life!

Now the Lord is the Spirit, and where the Spirit of the Lord is, there is freedom. And we, who with unveiled faces all reflect the Lord's glory, are being transformed into his likeness with ever-increasing glory, which comes from the Lord, who is the Spirit.

—2 CORINTHIANS 3:17–18

I pray that we all will have unveiled faces before the Lord, holding nothing back from the God o knows us better than we know ourselves.

Memorize the verse that spoke to you most significantly this week. Write it on an index card. rsonalize it and make it your own! Share with someone the areas that you need God's strength to ange and have that person pray for you.

Remember: Take the one most significant area and begin praying for God's plan of action; then obedient to His leading.

Don't Stop Lord

Lord
In asking You
To make me whole
I certainly didn't know
What I was in for.
You have ransacked me
Until I sometimes feel
There is nothing left.
But don't stop, Lord.
Please don't stop!
I'm trusting that the product
Will be worth the process.[8]

—RUTH HARMS CALKIN

Dear Lord,

Too often I look at others around me and calculate all the changes they need. I don't want to do that anymore. Instead, I want to busy myself looking at my own life and my own heart, actions, and attitudes. I ask You to change me from the inside out. Turn my world upside down if You need to so that my heart can be turned right side up! I am Yours. Fill me anew with Your precious Spirit, and give me the strength and grace to walk in the power of Your Spirit each and every day, instead of in my own feeble strength. Amen.

Journal Page

Don't stop Your good work in me, Lord …

_____

_____

_____

_____

_____

_____

_____

_____

_____

_____

_____

_____

_____

_____

_____

_____

_____

_____

_____

_____

_____

_____

KEY POINTS FROM LESSON 8

- God does for me that which I cannot do.
- His Spirit works "real change" in a surrendered life.
- Jesus makes the difference in whether I stay the same or move beyond myself.
- Every day I have a choice to commit to God the areas I am struggling with.
- God answers prayer.
- With God nothing is impossible.
- This life will have hardships.
- Jesus tells me to be of good cheer, for He has overcome all things.
- After I suffer awhile I will become stronger and more settled.
- Change happens in incremental steps—baby steps.
- We don't change overnight—it is a process.
- Growth is God restoring our life through His Son Jesus.
- The fruit of the Spirit is evident in a connected life.
- For fruit to grow there must be a pruning process.
- God is always working for the good in my life.
- I can trust Him and His strength on my behalf.

Love Has No Fear and Gives Me Hope

LESSON 9

*Each morning as you wake, there is a new opportunity to
"go out" building your confidence in God.*

—OSWALD CHAMBERS

Let us hold unswervingly to the hope we profess, for he who promised is faithful.

—HEBREWS 10:23

I will protect him, for he acknowledges my name.

—PSALM 91:14

ur world is full of challenges. It's littered with broken families, shattered dreams, addictions, pro-
scuity, crime. Jesus knew the world would be a hard place to live in. That is why He gave us so
any directives in advance. It is amazing how relevant the Bible is today, even though it was written
long ago.

In this lesson we will concentrate on hope. We will look at what it means to have hope, how to
ve hope, and how to battle today's hopelessness. The love of God will never leave us or forsake us.
is a constant anchor in this sea of life, and that means that in the midst of the storms we can
rn to have hope! It is hope in Christ that changes our fear factor.

 DAY ONE: HANG ON TO HOPE

1. Read Psalm 146. (If possible, read this psalm out loud.) Then underline the verses that **speaking to your heart and write your thoughts about them.**

• What does Psalm 146:3 tell you not to do?

• Have you put your trust in mortal men (husband, friends, children, relatives)? Why?

Too often we base everything on what people think of us. We put our trust in their belief syste and in their love, rather than in God's love.

> *We do not have to be successful or have to be pleasing to others to have a healthy*
> *sense of self-esteem and worth. That worth has freely and conclusively been given*
> *to us by God. Failure and/or the disapproval of others can't take it away![1]*
> —ROBERT MCGEE

• Who is blessed according to Psalm 146:5?

• What are some of the descriptions of the Lord in Psalm 146:5–6?

Psalm 146:7–10 paints what kind of picture of God's character?

Is this a God in whom you can have hope? Why, or why not?

> Hope: to want or wish for with a feeling of confident expectation
>
> Hopeless: to have no confident expectation

David began and ended this psalm with praise to God, because He is God who is so incredibly faithful that we can put all our hope in Him.

Are you in the middle of a seemingly hopeless situation? If so, what is it?

Sometimes our circumstances make it hard to have expectations and confidence. Yet we can live confidence when we are not moved by the circumstances around us but instead are encouraged and filled by our hope in God. God has plans for you—yes, He does!

Write out Jeremiah 29:11.

Read Hebrews 11:1–6. What are the key words or thoughts here?

Write out Hebrews 10:23.

5. Write out Hebrews 10:35.

• Why shouldn't you throw away your hope?

6. Read Hebrews 13:5–6. What won't God ever do to you?

• Is this a truth you need to hang on to? Explain.

Father,
Today I put my hope in You once again. And though I don't know what tomorrow brings, I do not fear. You have made my heart at peace with life and I thank You for that. Now, be my peace for all the little areas that try to pop up at me and drive me crazy! Amen.

 DAY TWO: HE IS MY PROTECTION

1. Read Psalm 139:5–10. (I know you keep reading Psalm 139, but bear with me. You will glad you did. Pay close attention to these words as if you have never read them before.)

What are these verses saying to you in regard to protection?

Draw a square box. Write your name in the center of the box.

In Psalm 139:5 I find relief. Just thinking that God goes before me, follows behind me, and places His hand on me gives me a picture of God enclosing me in His love. David even says in verse 6 that this is a fact wonderful to understand fully. He goes on to describe how God is always with him, and then he ends s thought beautifully in verse 10 when he says, "your hand will guide me, your right hand will hold me t." It is very important for us to understand that God does protect us and holds us in His hand.

Have you ever been struck by fear? Have you ever been stopped dead in your tracks by the kind fear that is heart-wrenching, stomach-achy, head-throbbing, and all-encompassing? What about xiety? It is another form of fear, worrying relentlessly over the details of the future or obsessing over outcome of any given situation. Have you known anxiety? When I am anxious for any length of ne, it seems as though my body goes down with me. Fear is awful!

Fear and anxiety have many variations and levels. Regrettably, I have mastered them all. I was a ild who was unusually fearful. As I grew up, my fears only magnified, while the veneer I wore to le the fears thickened. By the time I was in fifth grade, I was diagnosed with ulcers. Though my fears med unusual to me, and though I wanted out of them, I could not get over the hurdle of fear.

The evening I accepted Christ was the first glimpse I had that my fears could be conquered. For it moment, all fears were gone. The things I obsessed over and dreaded became so faded in the tance that I barely recognized them anymore. I felt free for the first time in almost eighteen years.

I wish I could tell you that my freedom from fear lasted indefinitely and that fear, worry, and xiety never raised their ugly heads again. But that's not the truth. I can say with confidence that as I ow in my relationship with Jesus, the story of fear in my life is playing out with a happy ending.

As I grow in relationship with the Father, my fears decrease. And as I understand the love of God vard me, fear, worry, and anxiety are much less frequent guests in my mind and body. My glimpse freedom upon salvation was a glimpse of what was to come as I grew to know God's love for me. In understanding His love and seeking Him, I am delivered from the bondage of worry. His love fills with confidence in the God who protects me and watches over me with loving care.

2. Write out the following verses.

Psalm 31:15

Psalm 37:24

John 10:28–29

• According to the verses above, where do you reside today? What does this mean?

        You cannot see the hands of God, but it is essential to believe by faith that they are there uphold you, protecting you, and guiding you.

3. Write out 1 John 4:18.

• What are the key words in 1 John 4:18?

Fear: alarm or agitation caused by
expectation or realization of danger;
dread or apprehension; to be frightened
or worried; to be timid; panic or terror

Instead of experiencing "NO FEAR," many of us "Know Fear" and struggle to understand why we st cannot get a grip on our fears.

Make a list of the things that you are most fearful of today.

Do you think God is big enough to take care of the things on your list that are holding you in the grip of fear? Why, or why not?

> *Two little girls were talking about God, and one said, "I know God does*
> *not love me. He could not care for such a tiny little girl like me."*
> *"Dear me, Sis," said the other girl, "don't you know that is just what God is for—to*
> *take care of tiny little girls who can't take care of themselves, just like us."*
> *"Is He?" said the first little girl, "I did not know that. Then I don't need to worry anymore, do I?"[2]*
> —HANNAH WHITALL SMITH

What are some of the characteristics of God's love that you have learned from the other lessons of this study that could help you understand why 1 John 4:18 says, "There is no fear in love"? (Refer to the description of love in 1 Corinthians 13.)

Why do you think love drives out fear?

First John 4:18 says, "The [one] who fears is not made perfect in love." This means that we have not atured in love as long as fear is present in us. It is a personal prayer of mine to understand the love

of God in such a way that fear won't be present in me. I realize that there are times of "normal" fe
such as apprehension when you see someone coming straight for your bumper through the rearvi
mirror or when you walk into your house after a burglary. We will all experience moments of fear n
and then. These kinds of fears cause us to wear seat belts and lock our doors. These fears act as t
guidelines for common sense.

The fear this verse talks about is the fear that torments and punishes you. The fear that things are r
going to be okay with you. The kind of fear that says, "There is not a God of love watching over me."
the kind of fear that has reduced God's love and protecti
to a fairy tale instead of the very real power that it is.

There is no fear in love [dread does
not exist], but full-grown (complete,
perfect) love turns fear out of doors
and expels every trace of terror! For
fear brings with it the thought of
punishment, and [so] he who is afraid
has not reached the full maturity
of love [is not yet grown into love's
complete perfection] (I John 4:18 AB).

Father,
I have no reason to be afraid, because
Your love guarantees that You will
not harm me. Please help me to have
a healthy awe of You, but never to be
afraid to come into Your presence to
talk to You. Amen.

 D{4}L   DAY THREE: NO FEAR IN LOVE

1. Write out the following verses.

Psalm 147:11

Proverbs 13:12

• Look up *deferred* in the dictionary. Write the definition here.

Look up Proverbs 13:12 in a different translation if possible. Can you relate to deferred hope? If so, how?

Write out Isaiah 40:31.

What are the key words in Isaiah 40:31?

What does Isaiah 40:31 mean to you?

This verse suggests that hope in God comes with promises. What are they?

Read Romans 5:1–5. What does peace with God mean?

According to Romans 5:1–5, where do you stand with God? What does this mean?

- In what do you rejoice? What does this mean?

- Why do you suppose character produces hope?

- What will hope not do? Why not?

All of us know about trials and sufferings, the things that produce character. I have experien
so much over the past ten years that I should be a *real character* by now! Many of you probably feel
same way. We tire of life's problems, partly because they are just plain hard and tire us out, and pa
because we need a new perspective on what good can come out of the hard stuff. But God's Word t
us to rejoice in our sufferings! Rejoice? How can we do that? Are we crazy? In denial?

NO! On the contrary, we are being led into truth by the Spirit of God, who teaches us the thi
of God. And one of those great things of God is that He is able to take the ugliness of our lives a
produce good things in us. After we have gone through suffering awhile, we develop more charac
and then character gives birth to *hope*—confident expectation. We can have confident expectat
because of the unfailing love of God that never changes.

One of the definitions of character is "a certain disposition." I like this definition because a
persevere, God develops in me a certain disposition of confidence in Him. As I learn of God's love
me, I develop a disposition of trust, security, and confidence. All my hope is in God.

Faith and hope go hand in hand.

Faith is the belief that God is real and that God is good. Faith is not a mystical experience or a
midnight vision or a voice in the forest…. It is a choice to believe that the one who made it all
hasn't left it all and that He still sends light into the shadows and responds to gestures of faith….
Faith is not the belief that God will do what you want. Faith is the belief that God will do

what is right. God's economy is upside down (or rightside up and ours is upside down!). God
says that the more hopeless your circumstances, the more likely your salvation. The greater your
cares, the more genuine your prayers. The darker the room, the greater the need for light.[3]
—MAX LUCADO

Lord,
Thank You for the promise of strength when I wait upon You. Amen.

 DAY FOUR: JOYFUL IN HOPE

Write out Romans 12:12.

This verse tells you to do three things. List them.

What does "be joyful in hope" mean to you?

I once knew a woman who seemed to skip through life. She had her share of challenges—breast
ncer and divorce after twenty-seven years, to name a few. Yet through her pain and heartache she
ntinued to smile and place her hope in God. She reminded me of someone skipping through a field
flowers without a care in the world. At first I thought she was just in *big denial* of her life's situation.
en I got to know her better.

I found she was a woman who had a relationship with God in a very real and practical way. Her
ationship with Him had been tested through some of the cruelest storms, yet she never gave up. She

was faithful in prayer. She prayed about all her needs every day. This was her method of survival, a it brought her great peace and joy.

Too many times, people look at Christians and think they would never want to be like us—worry more than they do! Unfortunately, it's true that we live like hopeless people much of the tin This is a sad statement of fact. Something should be different in a Christian's life, don't you think? I not talking about having it all together, because we aren't perfect and never will be. But something our disposition should point to the hope we have in God.

We should be living in the confidence that He loves us, that His very nature is love, and that nature is fixed, firm, and unchanging! Because of God's unchanging nature, we can rest in the fa of His faithfulness.

• On what is your hope fixed today? Why?

2. Write out Romans 15:4.

Scripture is meant to encourage us! It is intended to be a positive, not a negative. The world we l in makes it a negative with the attitude of "Those Christians can't do anything. They have so ma rules. They are no fun!"

Actually, the positive truth is that God came to give us a full life in Him. We can have plenty fun, plenty of joy, and plenty of peace. But we must have the encouragement of the Scriptures to tea us.

This week, memorize the verse that meant the most to you. Share your hope with others!

3. Look up Colossians 1:27–29 and write it in your own words.

The most wonderful thing we have to hope in is the fact that Christ is in us. He dwells within even though we are ordinary women. He is the hope that this life isn't the final call for us. His ergy works in and through us with power. This is awesome. Do you ever take for granted the t that Christ is in you? I know I do, but when I slow down, exhale, take a breath, and let it sink amazing things happen. I am not only filled with hope but also with joy, and definitely with *fidence* in Christ!

Our faith in God should make a difference in our daily lives. It should not be reduced to a nday school faith that only is brought out for church. We can proclaim to our unsaved friends and ghbors that we have a relationship with the living God, and that is why we are growing in hope d confidence. We are growing in the knowledge of His great love for us, and that gives us a new itude! Nothing is impossible when we have faith in God, and when we hope in Him.

Fear Not

Again and again, dear Lord,
I read Your words, "Fear not."
Surely You would not say it so often
If there were any reason to fear.
Nor would You command it so explicitly
If You could not keep me from fearing.
God, You have given me a Fear Not
For every puzzling circumstance
For every possible emergency
For every trial and testing
Real or imagined.
Yet I confess wasted hours—
Even days, dear Lord,
When fear clutches and clobbers me
Until I am physically and emotionally spent.
Lord, when David cried to You
You delivered him from all his fears.

On this gray-sky morning
I kneel before You with David's cry.
O my Father, I cannot believe
You would be less kind to me
Than You were to David.[4]

—RUTH HARMS CALKIN

 DAY FIVE: CAST YOUR CARES UPON HIM

1. What does 1 Peter 5:7 instruct you to do with your fears, concerns, and cares?

Do you know how to cast your cares upon the Lord? This concept is very basic. Cast means throw, to fling, to shed, to turn over. To cast your cares upon the Lord means you turn your wor. over to Him. You throw them all on His shoulders. This requires communication, which is pray Tell God everything—pour out your heart to Him. You can do this in a quiet place, or you can d driving down the freeway. Hey, if people can negotiate business deals over a cell phone on the freew you surely can negotiate handing your life's circumstances over to God while you are driving! You d even need a cell phone. Just dial 333—Jeremiah 33:3!

• How will you go about casting your cares upon the Lord?

2. Write out Jeremiah 33:3.

One of the greatest things we do not fully understand is God's love and concern for us. As we call it to Him, He will make us sure in His love!

Read Psalm 34:4–7. What does this passage say you are to do?

According to these verses, what is the result of seeking God?

How is your countenance affected by seeking God?

According to Psalm 34:4–7, where is the angel of the Lord?

Read Psalm 91. What is the main theme of this psalm?

According to this psalm, where are you supposed to dwell?

What does God command the angels to do for you?

• Read this psalm again—out loud. Let the meaning sink into your heart.

5. Read Psalm 23. If you think of this as a funeral text, ask the Holy Spirit to clear your mi
and speak the truth of this psalm to you personally in a new way. Write your thoughts.

• What does David say he will not fear? What does this mean?

Often we fear the worst. We seem to think good things are reserved for someone else who deserv
them, and we will just have to struggle through the hard knocks or the worst of life. This pattern

> We have this hope
> as an anchor for
> the soul, firm and
> secure (Heb. 6:19).

thinking is contrary to the Word of God, isn't it? Psalm 23:6 says, "Sure
goodness and love will follow me all the days of my life." These wor
were not written by someone fearing the worst! We cannot say, "I w
fear no evil," unless we have an understanding of "goodness and lov
following us all the days of our life.

Stop now and pray that God will make it real to you that He is your Shepherd. A shepherd
someone who takes care of the sheep. He feeds them, exercises them, protects them, and pulls the
back in when they've gone astray. God is your Shepherd.

David understood that God was his Shepherd and what that meant. Therefore he was able to sa
"I will fear no evil." Oh, that we may know God and His love in this same way, so that we too ca
confidently say, "Goodness and love will follow me."

Dear Lord,
When I think about Your love, I am filled with hope. My heart is full
and my mind at ease when the bigness of Your love is my focal point. If,
instead, I stop and look at myself or at others as a basis for happiness and
security, I fall flat on my face. I must be reminded over and over again that

You are my hope. You are the One in whom I will put my hope and trust. O precious Father, by the power of Your Spirit, fill me with the hope of heaven and the truth of eternity. May this hope keep me steady while I walk in the paths You have given me to tread here on earth. Amen.

Journal Page

- What has been the most meaningful part of this week's lesson for you?

_____

_____

_____

_____

_____

_____

_____

_____

_____

_____

_____

_____

_____

_____

_____

_____

_____

_____

_____

_____

_____

_____

KEY POINTS FROM LESSON 9

- In this world I will have troubles, fears, and heartache.
- Hope in Christ changes my fear factor to faith.
- God knows the plan He has for me.
- His plans are for good and not evil.
- Without faith in God, it's impossible to please Him.
- He will never leave me or forsake me.
- He protects me.
- He is my Shield of Protection.
- God is able to take care of me completely.
- Embracing His love for me drives out the fear that tries to invade my thoughts.

Love Lifts Me to New Heights

LESSON 10

Get up and do the next thing. What is the next thing? It is to trust Him absolutely and to pray on the basis of His redemption. Never let the sense of past failure defeat your next step.

—OSWALD CHAMBERS

Because your love is better than life, my lips will glorify you. I will praise you as long as I live.

—PSALM 63:3–4

everal years ago there was a popular song called "Up Where We Belong:"

> *Love lift us up where we belong,*
> *where the eagles cry, on a mountain high.*
> *Love lift us up where we belong*
> *far from the world we know.[1]*

We want to be lifted up above the gunk of life, not because we want to escape it entirely, but cause we know that our faith in Christ should be real enough to lift us above our circumstances into : land of faith, hope, love, and trust.

Unfortunately, not many of us are living consistently up where we belong. Don't get me wrong, s lesson is not about following man-made rules and regulations. On the contrary, this lesson is about owing God right up to the place that He has designed for us to live—the land of faith, hope, and derstanding His love.

When you are secure in a love relationship, you act securely. You do things that secure people do.

You accept, love, honor, and trust that the other partner in the relationship is doing the same. The le
of trust and security breathes a new kind of life into the relationship. On the other end of the sp
trum, when a relationship is not getting proper attention, those involved in the relationship experie
insecurity and fears. They behave in a way that is contrary to love and is instead selfish, immature, a
self-seeking. The lack of security in this kind of relationship discourages a bond with the other per
and instead encourages separation and disillusionment.

We must acknowledge that we are in a secure relationship with Christ. His Word says that noth
can separate us from the love of God, and no one can pluck us from our Father's hand. In this relati
ship it would be fitting for us to accept His Word, love Him with every part of us, and honor Him
trusting Him with all of our hearts. This kind of interaction on our part breeds in us the type of l
relationship with our Maker that promotes trust, security, and confidence. It lifts us to a better pla
It causes us to stretch to new heights in Him.

Now is the time to walk in that love relationship that God has already provided for us. It is ti
for His love to lift us up where we belong.

 **DAY ONE: HEARTS SET ON THINGS ABOVE**

**1. Read Colossians 2:20–22 and 3:1–3. Rewrite these passages, including the theme of each o
in your own words. Personalize them in a way that can be applied to your life.**

• According to Colossians 3:1, on what are you to set your heart and mind?

• Do you find this a struggle? Why, or why not?

Write out the following verses:

iah 48:17

overbs 3:5–7

Just how important is it to seek God on a daily basis? It is crucial! There is no way to have our inds set on things above if we are not in relationship with God. There is no way your marriage or any lationship will grow without attention and quality time. The more time spent, the more attention ven the relationship, the more it grows. Time spent with the Lord is like fertilizer to our hearts. It uses a rich crop to flourish within us. When we don't spend time with God, we are not focused on od and His plans but rather on us. In order to seek the things that are above and be lifted up where : belong, we need an attitude adjustment.

> *Words can never adequately convey the incredible impact of our attitude toward life. The longer I live the more convinced I become that life is 10 percent what happens to us and 90 percent how we respond to it. I believe the single most significant decision I can make on a day-to-day basis is my choice of attitude. It is more important than my past, my education, my bankroll, my successes or failures, fame or pain, what other people think of me or say about me, my circumstances, or my position. Attitude keeps me going or cripples my progress. It alone fuels my fire or assaults my hope. When my attitudes are right, there's no barrier too high, no valley too deep, no dream too extreme, no challenge too great for me.[2]*
>
> —CHARLES SWINDOLL

Lord,
Often I seek You last instead of first. I desire to have a heart and mind set on things above. Have Your way with me. Amen.

 **Day Two: A Refreshed Life**

1. Read Psalm 1:1–3. What do the following words mean in your life today?

Blessed is the [woman] who does not walk in the counsel of the wicked

[Her] delight is in the law of the LORD

On his law [she] meditates day and night

[She] is like a tree … which yields its fruit in season

Whatever [she] does prospers

2. Write out Colossians 2:6–7.

• What do the following phrases mean to you?
Continue to live in him

Rooted and built up in him

engthened in the faith

erflowing with thanksgiving

A few of the most wonderful by-products of understanding God's love are peace, security, and titude.

When we live with an "attitude of gratitude" in our everyday lives, we become women who live ording to a new set of rules. We are setting our hearts on Christ and His purposes, looking for the d in all things.

Gratitude is a buzzword these days. Isn't it interesting how something in the Bible can be taken d applied to life and then those promoting it get all the credit for its life-changing effects? The wers to all our heart's needs and longings are outlined within the practical principles of the Bible.

The Bible is full of principles to live by.

Gratitude, overflowing with thankfulness, and rejoicing in all things are just a few of the prinles. These principles, however, have the ability to change our lives by changing our attitudes and the y we view things. The way you view your life affects the way you live it!

Write out Psalm 116:7.

Lord,
It is so easy to see the negative instead of Your goodness. I am done with that.
Father, I want to be trained to see Your goodness in everything. Amen.

DAY THREE: DO ALL IN THE NAME OF THE LORD JESUS

1. Read Colossians 3:15–17. Rewrite each verse in your own words and personalize it. (Note t all three verses mention thankfulness and gratitude.)

verse 15

verse 16

verse 17

2. After all the instruction in Colossians 3, Paul goes on in chapter 4 to give final instructio Write out Colossians 4:2.

- According to Colossians 4:2, to what are you to devote yourself?

3. Again in the book of Philippians, Paul tells us to be thankful. In fact, he keeps repeating Write out Philippians 3:1.

- What do you think of that word *safeguard?* Why is rejoicing in the Lord a safeguard for you?

Write out Philippians 4:4. (Remember that *rejoice* means to be joyful.)

Father,

Be a safety latch to my mind and heart. Cause me to remember to praise You, giving thanks in all things. This is not natural for me, so I will need Your power working in me. Amen.

 Day Four: Find the Good and Dwell There

Read Philippians 4:6–8. What are the key words in these verses?

According to these verses, on what are you supposed to dwell?

Rewrite Philippians 4:6–8 in your everyday language.

Now spend some time memorizing this passage of Scripture.

Write out Philippians 4:9.

- According to this verse, what are you to put into practice?

- What will be the result of putting this into practice?

    The apostle Paul is a wonderful example for us to follow. We live in a world filled with heartac and disappointments—so did he. We live in a world where success and achievements mean putti confidence in our flesh and working hard to climb up the ladder—so did he. We live in a world wh our minds and our hearts are locked in the prisons of disappointments and shattered dreams—he w in prison too. Yet in all of these things he learned to be content (Phil. 4:11)—and so should we.

    Content: satisfied, happy, grateful.

Every woman lives in a tent: discontent or content.

    Where are you living today? Are you locked into seeing only the neg tive and the half-empty glass? Or are you grateful for the half-full glass th is set before you? In Philippians, Paul says that whatever we have seen h practice, we should also practice. One of the things he practiced was lea ing to be content. He had to learn contentment. It was not a natural trait or behavior, but rathe learned behavior.

3. Write out Ephesians 4:23–24.

- What is the key thought in these verses?

Lord,
Work contentment in me. I want to be satisfied with simple things. Amen.

 DAY FIVE: THE NEW PATTERN

Read Ephesians 5:1–2. What do the following words say to you?
imitators of God

dearly loved children

e a life of love

rist loved us and gave himself up for us

Once we have applied our hearts to understanding God's love for us, we must then apply our arts to learn what it means to live a life of love toward others.

Scripture tells us why we are to do that: because we are dearly loved and because Christ loved us d gave His life for us. We will be lifted to new heights as we learn to love those who do not love and yes, even those who have actually hurt us and wronged us. By the power of the Holy Spirit, od will work His love into our lives and give us the courage to obey Him.

The first step was pouring the right foundation to build on.

Understanding God's love is the right foundation.

Now by His Spirit, He can build the house and do His glorious work.

We each have many things to be thankful for despite our circumstances.

Make a list of the attributes of God's love that you can now see and appreciate.

• Make a list of all the people for whom you are thankful.

• Make a list of all the practical blessings God has given you in your everyday life.

God is stretching us, isn't He? He is stretching our values, belief systems, attitudes, and behavic

Stretch: to draw out
to the full length,
to extend from one
place to another

He is stretching us in the direction of love, joy, and thankfulness.
is calling us to say no to the lies and yes to God's truth. He does al
this for one purpose—that we might know Him and His love. Anc
we know that love more and more, He will bring our hearts and mi.
to places they have never been before.

I believe God wants to change us from glory to glory, just as His Word says. He stretches us
extends us from one place to another … draws out the best in us, making us all that He has desig
us to be. Stretching can be an exciting experience—it's all in the attitude!

And this is my prayer: that your love may abound more and more in knowledge
and depth of insight, so that you may be able to discern what is best and may be
pure and blameless until the day of Christ, filled with the fruit of righteousness
that comes through Jesus Christ—to the glory and praise of God.

—PHILIPPIANS 1:9

Dear Lord,
May Your love continue to lift me to higher places, places where I have never
been. May Your love so fill me that I will have no need for fear or anxiety, but
instead I will be able to trust in the love that never lets me go. Lord, lift me
up where I belong! Amen.

Journal Page

This week the Lord has shown me ...

_____
_____
_____
_____
_____
_____
_____
_____
_____
_____
_____
_____
_____
_____
_____
_____
_____
_____
_____
_____
_____
_____
_____
_____
_____

Key Points from Lesson 10

- I am no longer my own.
- My heart is God's—to be set on things above.
- I am to acknowledge God in all my ways.
- He loves me and will direct my paths.
- I am to be rooted and built up in Him.
- It's possible to refuse worry and anxiety.
- It's important to give my concerns and worries to God.
- Look for any good—and dwell there.
- Let peace rule.
- Contentment is a by-product of trusting in the love of God for me.

The Facts of Psalm 139

1. *God knows me; I am not a stranger to Him.*

2. *He understands me as an individual.*

3. *He is intimately acquainted with me.*

4. *He knows me well enough to know what I'll say next.*

5. *He is covering me; I am protected.*

6. *He is always with me.*

7. *I cannot separate myself from the love of God.*

8. *He leads me.*

9. *He holds my hand.*

10. *My life is not in darkness, but basked in His light.*

11. *He made me, putting all the pieces together.*

12. *I am a wonderful work of God's hand.*

13. *My life is a miracle.*

14. *My days have been ordained by God.*

15. *His thoughts are tender toward me.*

16. *He is always thinking of me.*

17. *God preserves me from day to day.*

18. *When I awake to start a new day, He is still with me.*

19. *I am alive by His design and plan.*

20. *He leads me in His will for me.*

Endnotes

NE: THE RELATIONSHIP OF LOVE

Genesis 2:25.

Genesis 3:10.

Roget's II, The New Thesaurus (Boston: Houghton Mifflin, 1980).

Chuck Smith, *Why Grace Changes Everything* (Eugene, OR: Harvest House, 1994), 7.

Charles Stanley, *The Savior's Touch* (Grand Rapids, MI: Zondervan, 1996), 67.

Smith, *Why Grace Changes Everything*, 1994, 13.

Hannah Whitall Smith and David Hazard, *Safe within Your Love* (Minneapolis: Bethany House, 1992), 39.

Tim Hansel, *You Gotta Keep on Dancin'* (Colorado Springs: ChariotVictor Publishing, 1995), 119.

O: GOD IS LOVE

Max Lucado, *Just Like Jesus* (Nashville: Word Books, 1998), 46.

Hannah Whitall Smith and David Hazard, *Safe within Your Love*, 1992, 85.

Oswald Chambers, *My Utmost for His Highest* (Grand Rapids, MI: Discovery House, revised 1992), devotion for January 22.

Andrew Murray, *Abide in Christ* (New York: Grosset & Dunlap, 1959).

REE: LOVE IS REAL AND PRACTICAL

Elisabeth Elliot, *Passion and Purity* (Grand Rapids, MI: Fleming Revell, 1984), 9.

A. W. Tozer, *Gems from Tozer* (Camp Hill, PA: Christian Publications, 1979), 35.

UR: LOVE CREATED ME

Robert McGee, *The Search for Significance* (Houston: Rapha, 1990), 27.

{

FIVE: LOVE ORDAINS MY DAYS

1 Chuck Smith, *Why Grace Changes Everything*, 1994, 56.

2 Ruth Harms Calkin, *Lord, I Keep Running Back to You* (Wheaton, IL: Tyndale House, Living Boo
1983), 11.

3 Oswald Chambers, *My Utmost for His Highest*, 1992, devotion for December 18.

SIX: LOVE IS MY FOUNDATION AND MY CONFIDENCE

1 Title poem from *Lord, Could You Hurry a Little?* by Ruth Harms Calkins, Pomona, CA, copyrig
1983. Used by permission. All rights reserved.

2 Barbara Johnson, *The Best of Barbara Johnson: Splashes of Joy in the Cesspools of Life* (New York: Ins
rational Press, 1996), 301.

3 Greg Laurie, *Every Day with Jesus* (Eugene, OR: Harvest House, 1993), 15.

4 Henri J. M. Nouwen, "Prayer and the Jealous God," *New Oxford Review*, Vol. LII, June 1985, quot
in Carol Kent, *Tame Your Fears* (Colorado Springs: NavPress, 1993), 9–10.

5 Robert McGee, *The Search for Significance*, 1990, 26.

6 McGee, *The Search for Significance*, 1990, 8.

7 Max Lucado, *Life Lessons with Max Lucado: Book of Hebrews* (Nashville: Word Publishing, 199
38.

8 Laurie, *Every Day with Jesus*. 1993, 36.

9 Oswald Chambers, *My Utmost for His Highest*, 1992, devotion for May 7.

SEVEN: LOVE CORRECTS ME

1 Billy Graham, *Unto the Hills* (as quoted in *Life Lessons with Max Lucado: Book of Hebrews*) (Dall
Word Publishing, 1986), 14.

2 Max Lucado, *Just Like Jesus*, 1998, 4.

3 Ruth Harms Calkin, *Lord, Could You Hurry a Little?*, 1983, 43.

4 Lucado, *Just Like Jesus*, 1998, x.

EIGHT: LOVE CHANGES ME

1 Max Lucado, *Just Like Jesus*, 1998, x.

2 Chuck Smith, *Why Grace Changes Everything*, 1994, 83.

Smith, *Why Grace Changes Everything,* 1994, 86.

Reinhold Niebuhr, "Serenity" in Rachel Callahan and Rea McDonnell, *Adult Children of Alcoholics* (Mahwala, NJ: Paulist Press, 1990), 149.

A. W. Tozer, *Gems from Tozer,* 1979, 8–9.

Andrew Murray, *Andrew Murray: The Best from All His Works* (Nashville: Nelson, 1988), 111.

Greg Laurie, *Every Day with Jesus,* 1993, 128–38

Ruth Harms Calkin, *Lord, Could You Hurry a Little?,* 1983, 28.

ONE: LOVE HAS NO FEAR AND GIVES ME HOPE

Robert McGee, *The Search for Significance,* 1990, 29–30.

Hannah Whitall Smith, *Living Confidently in God's Love* (Pittsburgh: Whittaker House, 1984), 37.

Max Lucado, *Life Lessons with Max Lucado: Book of Hebrews,* 1997, 79.

Ruth Harms Calkin, *Lord, Could You Hurry a Little?,* 1983, 84.

N: LOVE LIFTS ME TO NEW HEIGHTS

Will Jennings, "Up Where We Belong." Copyright 1982 by Famous Music Corporation and Ensign Music Corporation, New York, NY.

Charles R. Swindoll, *Strengthening Your Grip* (Nashville: Word, 1982). Used by permission of *Insight for Living,* Anaheim, CA 92806.

CPSIA information can be obtained at www.ICGtesting.com
Printed in the USA
BVOW07s2228010915

416085BV00018B/194/P

9 781434 768360